FROM ADVENT
TO HARVEST

Resources for worship in a complex world

Mark Geldard

First published in Great Britain in 2014

Society for Promoting Christian Knowledge
36 Causton Street
London SW1P 4ST
www.spckpublishing.co.uk

Copyright © Mark Geldard 2014

British Library Cataloguing-in-Publication Data
A catalogue record for this book is available from the British Library

ISBN 978–0–281–07093–0
eBook ISBN 978–0–281–07094–7

Typeset by Graphicraft Limited, Hong Kong
First printed in Great Britain by Ashford Colour Press
Subsequently digitally printed in Great Britain

eBook by Graphicraft Limited, Hong Kong

Produced on paper from sustainable forests

To Di
and our family

Contents

Acknowledgements

I am deeply grateful to the many people who have helped me in writing this book. I would especially like to mention my wife, Di, Angela Bate, Liz Jones, Nick Matthews, Pauline Shelton and also Rima Devereaux, Tracey Messenger and the staff at SPCK.

Introduction

This book is a collection of resources for use in worship throughout the year. It incorporates drama, various forms of visual interpretation, reflective readings, stories and music. Some of the items could be used in place of a sermon. Other items offer a programme for a whole service. In terms of the range of themes covered within the book, the Contents pages probably speak for themselves. Thus the primary focus in this introductory section is on practical matters.

The first point that I want to make here is that the resources in the book are all relatively simple to use. If you don't possess some of the skills needed to make use of an individual item – for example, particular IT skills – then it is pretty likely that somebody in your congregation will.

There are a number of specific practical matters that it might be helpful to touch on at this point.

USE OF SPACE

In putting these materials together, I have tried to be conscious of the varied character of church architecture. One or two of the dramas – particularly, perhaps, 'Christmas and Epiphany tableau' and 'Palm Sunday procession' – might require a full creative use of the varied spaces available to you: choir stalls, chancel steps, pulpit, lectern, aisles (or the comparable areas in less traditional or non-Anglican church buildings). However, if you are struggling for space, you will find that these items can accommodate some reduction in scale.

POWERPOINT

Four of the items in this book make use of PowerPoint presentations: 'Advent revisited', 'Upside-down people' Dramas 1 and 2, 'Your kingdom come' and 'The problem of suffering'. You will find the four presentations – fully prepared – on the website that accompanies the book. You just need to go to <www.advent2harvest.co.uk> and download the relevant resource. The website has been developed and will be maintained by the author and a specialist team in order to provide additional material for those using the book.

SIMULTANEOUS TEXT

If you are using 'Christmas: One of us', 'Pentecost: The Spirit of Jesus' or 'Harvest: A twenty-first-century celebration', you might like to consider supporting the *spoken word* through simultaneously displaying the text on a screen. You have the publisher's permission to scan the text for this purpose. However, please note that this permission is restricted to these three items.

HANDOUTS

In some worship contexts, it is, I feel, more appropriate to hand out leaflets containing key elements of a script than to display these on a screen. To facilitate this, you have permission to photocopy:

• the personal stories in 'Good Friday meditation: To the foot of the cross'

• the text of 'Complex lives'.

COPIES

In the case of some items, several people need to have a copy of the script. In this respect, you have the publisher's permission to make a reasonable number of copies of 'Advent revisited', 'The Pharisee and the tax collector', 'Palm Sunday procession', 'Pentecost: The Spirit of Jesus', 'Harvest: A twenty-first-century celebration', 'Upside-down people' Dramas 1 and 2 and 'Gazumped!'

MUSIC: HYMNS, SONGS, BACKGROUND MUSIC …

I make no claims to be an expert in musical matters. From time to time, I have suggested particular items of music but you might well have better ideas of your own. However, I do believe that we need to be adventurous in making selections of music that are both inspirational and inclusive – embracing the traditional and the contemporary, the classical and the popular.

VOICES

There is sometimes a question about whether it is best to use one voice or more than one in the delivery of Bible readings, reflective readings, narration, etc. There are arguments on both sides here. Using a number of voices certainly helps to maintain freshness. But, equally, the use of a single voice can sometimes facilitate continuity of emphasis and meaning.

I have made occasional specific suggestions in cases where I believe there are particular benefits to be had from deploying more than one 'reader'.

I have greatly enjoyed developing resources of this form in my own ministry – among fairly typical Anglican congregations made up of a broad mix of people.

Perhaps one of the greatest joys of using this type of material is the way in which it provides so many opportunities for members of the congregation to harness their own particular creativity, skills and enthusiasms – in areas such as IT, photography, music, organization and drama.

Part 1

SEASONAL MATERIAL

ADVENT REVISITED

INTRODUCTION

'Advent revisited' starts with an exploration of the uniqueness of the human story and proceeds to consider what it means for this story to have *an outcome*. It brings together reflective readings and photographic images; it could be used for a meditation during the early part of Advent – or perhaps as a reflective sermon.

PREPARATION

Photographic images: to complement and interpret the text

This item includes a PowerPoint presentation. To download the fully prepared presentation, please go to <www.advent2harvest.co.uk> (see page 1 above). The contents are set out below.

Image 1   teenagers in a classroom

Image 2   somebody using a microscope in a laboratory

Image 3   endless rows of books in a major library

Image 4   a person operating a computer

Image 5   a colourful embroidery

Image 6   handmade furniture

Image 7   composite image – a satellite in orbit and a spectacular bridge

Image 8   composite image – musician, film star, writer

Image 9   photographs depicting a range of human emotions

Image 10   children playing

Image 11   a couple embracing

Image 12   work colleagues in a meeting

Image 13   composite image – Houses of Parliament, the International Red Cross

Image 14   a slide with the following words arranged on it: truth-telling, bullying, euthanasia, justice, marriage, gossip, taxation …

Image 15   the sea

Image 16   Stonehenge

Image 17   worship in a distinctive tradition

Image 18   firefighters of 9/11

Image 19   composite image – made up of a selection from Images 1–18

Image 20   composite image – as 19: a further selection

Image 21   a cereal crop ready to be harvested

Image 22   a portrait of a 'lived-in' face.

Reflections

It would probably be helpful to have at least two readers.

You might like to display the passage of Scripture, the meditative prayer and the closing response (all in Reflection 3) on the screen. You have the publisher's permission to do this. These three portions of the text, and the short medley of music that falls halfway through Reflection 1, are all included in the PowerPoint presentation on the website that accompanies the book.

Music

You could also consider providing background music for the two periods of personal reflection.

ADVENT REVISITED

REFLECTION I

Reader I   Think, for a moment, about people
...about humanity, humankind.
Consider the ways in which we live ... the things we do,
our particular qualities and attributes.

Consider, for example, our capacity to think ... to learn ... to discover
... and to accumulate knowledge.

Image 1

Image 2

Image 3

Image 4

Consider our many forms of creativity ... including our technology.

Image 5

Image 6

Image 7

Image 8

(A very short medley of two or three different styles of music could be played at this point.)

Or, reflect on the character of human emotions ...
their complexity, their range ...
their delicacy ... and their ferocity.

Image 9

Think about the character of human relationships ...
their diversity ...
their depth ... and their subtlety.

Image 10

Image 11

Image 12

Image 13

Think about our capacity for moral life

Image 14

... and for spiritual awareness.

Image 15

Image 16

Image 17

Or, reflect on our potential for the most extraordinary altruism, self-sacrifice, heroism.

Image 18

Pause for personal reflection (music)

REFLECTION 2

Image 19

Reader 2   When we reflect in all these different ways about people ...
about the ways in which we think ...
about the character of our feelings,
about what we do ... and what we make
... we cannot but be struck by the uniqueness of humankind.
No wonder the psalmist declares that the human being is little less than a god.[1]

It is true that we, the members of the human race, often abuse our freedom
– sometimes in the most terrible of ways.
It is also true that, for a multitude of reasons, many of us live significantly below our
full potential.
And daily life is full of struggles and complications.

Yet there remains something truly compelling about humanity.

Image 20

There is a distinctiveness about the people of the earth.
We possess qualities and capabilities far, far beyond those possessed by any other creatures.
Intellectually, emotionally, socially, artistically – we stand apart.
In respect of our moral and spiritual awareness – we stand apart.
There are no other species like us.
None that even come close to us.
To the eye of faith,
our distinctiveness reflects a unique gift in creation,
a unique endowment
... the very image of God within us.

Brief pause

Reader 1   In our understanding of the human race, we should not pitch faith against science.
Faith and science are not enemies.
Science explains some of the processes that have helped to shape human
development ...
whereas faith tells us about God's creative desire.
Faith tells us *why* there is a creature that has developed such a remarkable life.
Faith sees a creature capable of sharing in the work of creation.
Faith sees a creature capable of responding to its Creator.[2]

Pause for personal reflection (music)

REFLECTION 3

Image 20 (continues)

Reader 2   A key dimension of Christian teaching is that humankind is distinctive … special
…the crown of creation.[3]

And thus the story of humankind is a unique story.

It is the story of a creature exercising freedom
– the freedom to choose
…between different ways of living
…between right and wrong.

It is, as we have seen, an unparalleled story of
creativity and skills,
of emotional depth and social development,
and of spirituality.

But it is also a story with
its shame … and destructiveness
…and God hung on a human cross.

Brief pause

Image 21

The Christian faith also teaches us that this story has an outcome.
The writers of the New Testament actually use a variety of images and concepts
to portray the outcome of the human story. But one of the themes that weaves
its way through these various strands is that of completion.[4]
Christ's work will come to fruition …
God will bring an order of fulfilment and wholeness out of the fractures, highs and
lows, strivings and fragilities of this present life.

There is much in this aspect of Christian teaching that is not easy to understand and interpret.
And our imaginations strain and struggle to cope with ideas that are, by their very
nature, beyond anything that we have ever experienced.

Image 22

But Christian faith invites us to live in confident hope …
including the hope that our own lives will ultimately come to completeness.
This vision of 'life beyond this life' is expressed in these verses from the book of Jude
in the New Testament. You might like to reflect on them for a moment.[5]

Display verses on screen – see Introduction.

Reader 1   To him who is able to keep us from falling,
and to present us
faultless …
and joyful
to the one God, our Saviour,
be glory and majesty,
now and for ever.
Amen.

Brief pause for thought

        Consider also the words of this meditative prayer.

Display prayer on screen:

Reader 2   And then, Lord,
        all that I truly am …
        all that makes me the real me …
        all that you have already wrought in me …
        all that is the best in me
        will be brought to fulfilment
        and I will, at last, be whole.

Brief pause for thought

        We draw towards a conclusion with a centuries-old prayer that is based on words of St Augustine.

        Almighty God,
        you have made us for yourself,
        and our hearts are restless
        till they find their rest in you.
        Teach us to offer ourselves to your service,
        that here we may have your peace,
        and in the world to come may see you face to face;
        through Jesus Christ our Lord.
        Amen.[6]

Closing response (screen)

        Yours, Lord, is the power to create
        … and to complete.

All   **Praise to you, O Lord.**

CHRISTMAS AND EPIPHANY TABLEAU

INTRODUCTION

The first objective of the tableau is to show how the love of Jesus embraced people of every kind – whatever their social, political or racial background and whatever their personal circumstances. In order to achieve this objective, the tableau utilizes two dramatic devices.

1 The tableau scene ultimately takes us beyond the visits of the shepherds and the wise men to incorporate other individuals who came face to face with Jesus during his earthly life.

2 It highlights the social diversity of the people with whom Jesus engaged by putting them into contemporary dress.

The second objective of the tableau is to encourage members of the congregation to consider the different ways in which God still comes to us today.

The tableau can stand alone but here I have set it in the context of a simple service.

PREPARATION

Music

The occasion provides a number of opportunities for inspirational music: congregational carols, choir, music group, organ, CD …

I have made one or two suggestions in the text.

The tableau

The scene for the tableau is a contemporary space of a functional character – for example, a storeroom or an outhouse. Some simple artefacts should suffice to create this impression – stacked boxes or crates, bucket and mops …

The following characters are suggested:

Mary: a young woman, looking pale and tired

Joseph: mid twenties, wearing, for example, a BT bib

A local woman: helping Mary

A middle-aged man looking on: perhaps the owner of the building where Jesus has been born.

First visitors: four or five low-paid shift workers – rough and ready in both appearance and demeanour. The group could include men and women.

Scholars: suggestions –

> An elderly man – a dusty academic carrying a briefcase

> A young woman – elegant, modern, carrying a laptop or a tablet

> An older woman (power-dresser) or dapper middle-aged man.

Characters from Jesus' adult life:

> A soldier in uniform, and with an air of composure, authority

> A clergyman or clergywoman – wearing suit and clerical collar

> The 'woman of ill repute' in Luke 7.36ff. Her appearance (clothing, hairstyle …) obviously needs to be thought through with both imagination and sensitivity.

> An ill or frail person – poor, dishevelled

> An entrepreneur – wealthy, confident.

Two people who will enter the tableau from their seats in the congregation. They will represent the congregation in the tableau.

You will also need a reader/narrator.

Use of space

If you are working in the context of traditional architecture, you will obviously need to make creative use of the choir stalls, chancel steps and areas around the pulpit and lectern. However, if space is very limited, it is possible to make a small reduction in the number of characters.

Joseph, the local woman and the owner enter the tableau from the front of the church. All the other participants enter through the congregation.

Once within the tableau, the characters focus on the Christ Child and maintain a standing or sitting position. The one exception is at the very outset when some actions are quite a useful way of setting the scene.

CHRISTMAS AND EPIPHANY TABLEAU

INTRODUCTION

Welcome

Congregational carol

Christmas bidding prayer

Bible reading: Luke 2.1–16

Choir piece, or alternative musical item

Bible reading: Matthew 2.1–12

Congregational carol

THE TABLEAU

As the music of a carol is played quietly, the lighting is enhanced in the area where the tableau is to take place. (Suggested carol: 'Infant holy, infant lowly …')

Mary is seated. She has a blanket around her and her feet up.

Joseph enters. He puts his arm around Mary, hugs her and kisses her on the forehead. He then arranges some furniture: a seat, so that he can sit next to her, and a box which looks as if it could serve as a crib. Joseph then sits down next to Mary.

A local woman brings 'the baby' and places 'him' in Mary's arms. She too gives Mary a gentle hug.

The owner enters, hovering on the sidelines.

Narrator   This is the season for celebration.
We celebrate
with gifts and gatherings,
with leaf and light,
that God has come to us.

Of course, God is always everywhere.
He is not limited by physical location.
Yet, in a very special sense, God came to us two thousand years ago.
He came to us …
he reached out to us …
by becoming one of us
… born as a baby at Bethlehem.

Brief pause

When God,
in Jesus,
was born at Bethlehem,
he was among people of every kind.

Jesus' own mother was a young woman from an ordinary family,
living in an ordinary provincial town.
Joseph was a decent and caring lad
with a good skill to his name.
Jesus' birth in Bethlehem became an emergency;
and so he was born in an outhouse
with the help of kindly locals.

Very briefly: further strains of 'Infant holy, infant lowly …'

When Jesus was born in Bethlehem,
his presence among us was announced first to a group of low-paid shift workers,
a rough and ready bunch
who made their way down from the chill of the hills.

The shift workers come through the congregation and take up their places in the tableau.

As a toddler,
Jesus was attended by a group of scholars –
eminent specialists who studied documents and charts,
ideas and events.

The scholars make their way through the congregation and enter the tableau. They lay down their gifts.

Music: choir piece, instrumental

God, in the person of Jesus, walked the dust of the earth two thousand years ago.
He came to the people of Palestine.
He came to
fishermen and solicitors,
clergy and street girls,
soldiers and entrepreneurs.

He came to the ordinary and the extraordinary,
to the confident and the desperate,
to Jews and Samaritans,
to political collaborators and militant nationalists.

There were none who were his special type,
and none who were not his type.
He reached out to them all,
whatever their colour or gender or creed,
whatever their circumstances,
whatever their past.

The soldier, clergyman/woman, 'woman of ill repute', ill/frail person and the entrepreneur now make their way through the congregation, one at a time, and enter the tableau.

He loved them all.
He offered them his friendship and forgiveness . . .
and he challenged them . . .
taught them, dared them,
to live by his way of love and peace,
and to trust him.

He called them to join his movement –
to work with him in healing the world's divisions and brokenness.

Music: choir piece, instrumental

This is the season for celebration.
We celebrate
with gifts and gatherings,
with leaf and light,
that God has come to us.

He came to us in Bethlehem
and, through his Spirit, he still comes to us today.
He comes to each one of us . . .
whoever we are,
whatever our circumstances,
whatever our past.

He comes to us and he calls us.
His call is all about us
and within us.

When we yearn for a deeper stillness at the centre of our lives …
when we yearn to be part of something bigger than ourselves …
this is God calling us.

When we need to know that we are forgiven …
when we need to put the burden down …
when we are struggling to forgive ourselves …
this is God calling us.

At this point, the first congregational representative leaves his or her seat and enters the tableau.

When I know that I need to renew my commitment to somebody close to me …
When I want to forgive a colleague …
or even just want to want to …
When I feel challenged to go the extra mile in my daily tasks …
this is God calling me.

Brief pause

When I find myself unusually stirred
by the tear on the cheek of the starving child on my TV screen …
or by the aimlessness of the kids who hang around the bus stop …
or by the awful fate of a prisoner of conscience in a faraway jail …
perhaps this is God calling me.[1]

The second congregational representative enters the tableau.

PRAYER

God, who was placed in straw,
Jesus, king and servant,
you call us to live within the embrace of your love.
May we find our peace in you.

God, who gazed with a child's awe at the presents brought by the wise men,
Jesus, king and servant,
you call us, as you called the people of Palestine, to be part of your movement –
to work with you in healing the world's divisions and brokenness.
We know that we cannot respond to all of the world's needs,
but may we always be open to your calling within us.
Amen.

CONCLUSION

Congregational carol

(Suggestion: the words of 'In the bleak mid-winter' are very appropriate at this point.)

The congregation needs to be seated for this carol.

Dispersal

As the congregation sings, the characters in the tableau disperse.

Mary and Joseph leave from the back of the tableau.

The other characters exit informally, but silently, through the congregation. As they leave, they share gentle greetings with each other: a pat on the shoulder, a handshake on the move, a smile and a nod of the head. One of the characters assists the ill/frail person.

Collect or closing prayer, and blessing

Congregational carol

CHRISTMAS: ONE OF US

INTRODUCTION

'One of us' combines reflective readings, music and visual interpretation in exploring a theme that lies at the heart of the Christmas message.

The item could be used in place of a sermon in a variety of contexts during the Christmas season, including carol services and midnight Holy Communion.

PREPARATION

Music

I have suggested that music is played between the readings. I would recommend using one piece of music – with a strong recurrent theme – throughout. For example, 'Laudate Dominum' (Taizé chant) – music only, on organ.

Visual interpretation

Four very large cardboard boxes are wrapped in Christmas gift paper. Each of the boxes is brought to the front of the church at a particular point during the reading of the text (see script). They are eventually arranged to form the shape of a cross.

Readings

You might like to consider supporting the *spoken word* by displaying the text on a screen as it is read. If so, please see the introductory section ('Simultaneous text') on page 1.

ONE OF US

When God reached out to us that first Christmas,
he didn't hold back.
He didn't simply, as it were, send a message.
Rather, he took the ultimate step …
he became one of us
… born as a baby at Bethlehem.

And when God became one of us,
he did not do it gingerly … safely, self-protectively, selectively.
No, God placed himself right in the thick of it …
right in the thick of human life.
He embraced the vulnerabilities of being human.

He exposed himself to the frailties of being a baby at a time when medicine
was still pretty primitive.
God's cot was a feeding trough.
The maternity suite was an animal shed.
His parents were inexperienced and under pressure.

Later he knew the turbulence, the hormones, of adolescence,
and grew to adulthood.

This was no aloof, detached God.

Selected music to be played for the first time – fairly briefly

In adult life, God, in Jesus,
experienced the richness of human solidarity.
He enjoyed companionship and laughter.

But the world he embraced also contained much that was brutal.
It was a time of corrupted politics and divisive religion.
Yet Jesus never remained on the social fringes.
He did not stay in secure places.
He lived his life right in the eye of the human storm.
He was constantly surrounded by the dangerous and the contagious.
These were violent times and he eventually died a violent death.

Music – briefly

In northern climes,
Christmas is loved by many as a season of cosiness –
of warmed and brightly lit interiors
set against the winter dark and dank.
This is part of its magic …
and light in the darkness is what we are celebrating.
But while there was joy in God's experience of human life,
it was never cosy.

For God also opened himself up to the chill of our dark side ...
to our meanness and our menace.

Music: during which the first box is brought forward and placed as a vertical upright.

Christmas is God being born as a baby
and living among us;
because, by living among us,
God could demonstrate the depth of his desire to befriend us.

And by living among us,
God could feel what we feel ... the full range of our emotions:
God could understand,
from within,
what it is like to be a person.

And by living among us,
God could show us how to live;
because Jesus did not only show us what God is like,
he also showed us what human life could be like.

Music: during which the second box is brought forward and placed on top of the first box as a further vertical upright.

By choosing to live among us,
as one of us,
God could enter right into the heart of humanity –
right into the depths of its glory and its grubbiness.
For only from there,
only from within the very pulse of human life,
could the story of its renewal begin.

Music: during which the third box (crosspiece) and the fourth box (top piece) are brought forward and arranged to complete the cross – in interpretation of the preceding section of text.

God calls us to be Christmas people too.

On the factory floor and in the office,
in the boardroom and the council chamber,
on building sites, websites, tense first nights,
in the local league football team, the gardening club, the WI ...
there, wherever we are,
God calls us to be Christmas people.

In the school, the hospital, the police station, the church,
in finance houses and public houses,
in high places and humble places ...
there, wherever we are,
God calls us to be Christmas people.

In the street, the village, the tower block,
among the orphaned, the poor and the scared ...
there, wherever we are,

God calls us to be
peacemakers,
channels of quiet compassion,
bearers of hope.
There, wherever we are,
God calls us,
in big ways and in small ways,
to be sources of integrity … cohesion … justice …
For thus we are instruments of God's purposes in the world.
Thus we are servants of God's kingdom.

Music: for the final time

PRAYER

Lord, we thank you that you chose to live among us,
as one of us.
Strengthen us by your Spirit.
Give us the courage, the vision and the love
to be Christmas people too.
So may we be instruments of your purposes in the world.
This we ask in Jesus' name.
Amen.

DRAMA FOR LENT: THE PHARISEE AND THE TAX COLLECTOR

INTRODUCTION

'The Pharisee and the tax collector' uses drama to set the scene for an exploration of the contemporary relevance of Jesus' parable.

Its use would be appropriate in services that focus on the Lenten themes of self-examination and repentance.

The material divides into four parts:

1 the drama

2 some brief observations on the meaning of the parable

3 a short reflection on the theme of self-examination and repentance

4 three reflections that explore some wider implications of Jesus' parable.

Parts 1–3 are arranged as a sequence and constitute the core material. The reflections in the final section should be seen as extra *optional* material. You might, for example, like to choose one of them to follow on from parts 1–3.

Part 3 could, with minor amendments, serve as a short stand-alone resource for the Lenten season.

PREPARATION

The parable is found in Luke 18.9–14.

The drama has a very simple format. There are ten voice parts altogether: two readers, Jesus, a Pharisee, a tax collector and five contemporary worshippers.

No period dress is required.

Canned laughter is suggested at one point in the text. This is, of course, not an essential ingredient! For easy access to canned laughter, go to <www.advent2harvest.co.uk>.

THE PHARISEE AND THE TAX COLLECTOR

The two readers and Jesus take their places at the front of the church. The physical positions of the three characters need to present a clear distinction between the roles of the readers and that of Jesus.

Reader 1   In the church year, we are in the season of Lent. It is a time for self-examination: for looking at our own lives in the light of Christ's teaching.
Listen to this parable told by Jesus.[1]

Jesus   There were two men who went up to the temple to pray. One was a religious leader, a Pharisee.

The Pharisee enters. He walks confidently up the main aisle of the church to the very front and stands in a central position.

Jesus   The other man was a tax collector.

The tax collector enters. He walks up the main aisle of the church but stops halfway.

Jesus   The Pharisee stood apart by himself and prayed:

Pharisee   I thank you, God, that I am not greedy, dishonest or an adulterer like everybody else. I thank you that I am not like that tax collector behind me. I fast two days a week, and I give you a tenth of all my income.

Jesus   But the tax collector stood at a distance and would not even raise his face to heaven. He prayed:

Tax collector   God, have pity on me, a sinner!

Jesus   I tell you, the tax collector, and not the Pharisee, was in the right with God when he went home. For all who make themselves great will be humbled, and all who humble themselves will be made great.

Pause.

Jesus, the Pharisee and the tax collector depart.

Reader 2   In church congregations today, feelings of superiority and self-righteousness might perhaps focus on different sorts of issues from the ones highlighted in Jesus' parable.

Contemporary Worshipper 1 enters followed by Contemporary Worshipper 2.

They walk down the main aisle to the front of the church and kneel down – either on the chancel steps or at a similar location.

Contemporary Worshipper 1   Lord, I do wish that the people in our church could be more committed. The vicar's priorities aren't all they could be. And what about Bill here, kneeling next to me. He's a nice enough chap ... in his own way. But you'd think that now he's retired, he could help out rather more. I mean, what else has he got to do all day? We need all the help we can get.

Pause

Contemporary Worshipper 2   Lord, I know I can be a real pain in the neck sometimes. Help me to be much more aware of Ann's feelings. I feel as if the way I go about things at home often doesn't do much for her confidence.

Pause

Contemporary Worshippers 1 and 2 depart.

Contemporary Worshipper 3 enters, followed by Contemporary Worshipper 4. They kneel down.

Contemporary Worshipper 3   Lord, I'm so grateful that I know how to discipline my children properly. Not like Sandra here. By what I hear, her two are more than a handful.

Pause

Contemporary Worshipper 4   Lord, I realize I was in the wrong yesterday. Help me to say sorry for what I said.

Pause

Contemporary Worshippers 3 and 4 depart.

Contemporary Worshipper 5 enters.

Contemporary Worshipper 5   Lord, I thank you that I'm not like so many people with all their feelings of superiority. Not me; I don't feel superior to other people in any way at all!

Contemporary Worshipper 5 departs.

Pause

OBSERVATIONS

Reader 1 Jesus' parable about the Pharisee and the tax collector presents us with a terrifying picture of self-righteousness. But there can be very few of us who don't sometimes find ourselves looking down on other people.

Reader 2 Yet Jesus was particularly tough on the sins of self-righteousness and religious snobbery and superiority.

He was fierce in his criticism of the hypocrites who prayed on street corners so that everybody would think how spiritual they were.[2]

And Jesus said that God would judge us using the same standards that we use when we are being judgemental about others.[3]

Reader 1 Sometimes, Jesus used humour to get his point across. He told a joke along the following lines.

Reader 2 Hey, don't you know that it's dangerous to try to get a speck of grit out of somebody's eye when you've got a great big plank in your own!![4]

Canned laughter

Reader 1 The parable about the Pharisee and the tax collector shows us just why Jesus was so tough on self-righteousness. It explains why he saw it as such a dangerous cast of mind. For self-righteousness – and feelings of religious superiority – undermine both our relationship with God and our relationships with each other.

The Pharisee was actually so distracted by his superficial sense of superiority to others that he could not even start to see his own faults and need for forgiveness.

In stark contrast, the tax collector was able to ask for, and receive, God's forgiveness.

Pause

REFLECTION

Reader 2   For some of us, the natural tendency is to be too easy on ourselves. When we act badly, we tend to let ourselves off the hook. We can always find some sort of an excuse. Sometimes we might even resort to the ultimate excuse . . . 'I'm afraid that's just the way I am.'

        Perhaps we need to make more time for self-examination . . . and to consider how our actions and attitudes affect others. Perhaps we need to allow the teachings of Jesus to penetrate our lives a little more.

Reader 1   For others of us, the natural tendency is to be too hard on ourselves. We always see our motivations in the worst possible light. When we are with other people, we find ourselves thinking . . . 'If you really knew me, you wouldn't like me very much.'

        We feel like fakes – always on the verge of being found out. We very easily start to blame ourselves, even on occasions when we've done nothing wrong.

        We need to see ourselves as loved by God. We need to be able to recognize the good points in our lives.

Reader 2   So what is our natural tendency?

        To be too easy on ourselves?

        To be too hard on ourselves?

        Of course, life is complicated. Perhaps we're too easy on ourselves in some areas of our lives and too hard on ourselves in other areas.

Silence: for a short period of reflection.

Reader 2   May God give to each one of us the precious gift of balance . . . so that we may not be too easy on ourselves, but not too hard on ourselves either.

ADDITIONAL MATERIAL

Reflection 1

Reader   There is a form of goodness, holiness, piety – or supposed goodness, holiness, piety – that is, as the phrase puts it, 'holier than thou'. It makes other people feel uncomfortable, inferior … judged. It can be rather threatening and intimidating.

Contrast this with the holiness of Jesus. He was a man of deep spiritual devotion and prayerfulness, and of a pure goodness. Yet people felt that they could approach him. To him, they came … among them the shamed, the social outcasts … the fearful. They knew that Jesus would welcome them and understand them. They knew that he would treat them as people and get to the heart of their needs.

Of course, there were those who disagreed with Jesus' message. And there were those who felt that his message threatened their power and position.

But there is something so profoundly appealing about the character of Jesus:

He was truly holy … yet totally approachable.

He was God in human form … yet wholly accessible.

Reflection 2

Reader 1   In our society, many people – and in particular, perhaps, many younger people – are suspicious of religion. They see religions as being divisive and exclusive. They feel that for them to embrace a religion would be an act of separation. It would put a divide – a gap, a chasm – between themselves and others. It would feel like signing up to a tribal mentality.[5]

Reader 2   The tribal mentality was thick on the ground in Jesus' day.

Take the relationship between Jews and Samaritans, for example.

The Samaritans were members of a different religious community with their own distinctive beliefs. And in Jesus' time, many Jews looked down on people from Samaria. But Jesus challenged this sort of tribal superiority. And in his famous parable – the Parable of the Good Samaritan – he chose a Samaritan to be his role model for love in action.[6]

Reader 1   Lord, help me to live out my faith in a way that makes it absolutely clear that I value all people – whatever their religion, non-religion, race or class – as being of equal worth.

Reflection 3

Reader 1   The Bible is a gift to us – to guide us in faith and life.

But think about what the Bible is like. It does not consist of several sheets of A4 with four or five neat points for us to follow. In some ways, the Bible is more like a small library with its rich assortment of different types of literature – history, poetry, teachings, letters, biographies, stories, practical wisdom … Within the Bible's varied writings, there is a definite unity in terms of the big themes and the great truths which we repeatedly encounter. But within the underlying unity of the Bible, we also find diversity. We find a variety of perspectives, emphases, approaches …

Take worship, for example.

Reader 2   In the Bible, we find different ways of worshipping God. Some of these forms of worship were structured and had been committed to writing. Others were characterized by spontaneity. The Bible does not lay down one way of worshipping God. It gives us room to move. Unity is not uniformity.

Reader 1 Or consider the fact that, at the beginning of the New Testament, we find not one Gospel, but four. And each of the four Gospels is distinctive. Each one has its own definite flavour – its own particular emphases and understandings.

Reader 2 The Bible needs to be interpreted so that it can be applied to our lives today. But, as we seek to understand the meaning of Christian faith in today's world, there needs to be great humility and respect for each other. And above all, there needs to be reverence for the *bigness* of God:

God is too big to be contained in the vision of any one person, too big to be contained in the perspectives of any one tradition or group or denomination.

PALM SUNDAY PROCESSION

INTRODUCTION

'Palm Sunday procession' was written to convey something of the poignancy of Palm Sunday. It is a day when we focus on the triumphal entry of Jesus into Jerusalem and the acclamation he received, but we know that a few days later he was rejected and crucified. The poignancy and irony are expressed here through the interplay between the three groups that make up the drama.

- The participants in the procession: they represent the members of the crowd who greeted Jesus as he entered Jerusalem – those who acclaimed him, cheered and chanted, put down clothes and branches.

- The observers:

  Those people who cheered and chanted were united in acclaiming Jesus, although we should not assume that they all shared identical expectations of him. There were also some people present who were unhappy about what was happening. Luke records that some of the Pharisees were angered by such wild scenes of celebration and urged Jesus to calm things down. However, we can imagine that there must have been others there who were more on the sidelines – those who wondered about Jesus. Who was he? Why was he entering the city in this way? What was his mission? These people are represented in the drama by two observers who provide the dialogue.

- The congregation: members of the congregation participate through singing selected verses from Palm Sunday hymns at specific points during the procession. In this way, they fulfil a particular role in the drama. They are the interpreters of the event. They know what happened next. They interpret the significance of Jesus' entry into Jerusalem from the perspective of Christian understanding.

'Palm Sunday procession' could be used in place of a sermon in most forms of service. It was written for use inside but could be easily adapted for use in a Palm Sunday outdoor service or walk.

PREPARATION

Bible reading

All four Gospels include an account of Jesus' triumphal entry into Jerusalem: Matthew 21.1–11; Mark 11.1–10; Luke 19.28–40; John 12.12–16.

Matthew makes the most explicit reference to the symbolic significance of the way in which Jesus entered the city – mounted on a donkey.

'Here is your king, who comes to you in gentleness, riding on a donkey, on the foal of a beast of burden.'[1]

The procession

- There is no need for any form of period dress but the procession ought to be colourful and festive.

- It adds a great deal to the atmosphere if some members of the procession are playing musical instruments. For example, you could have somebody with bongo drums beating out a basic rhythm for the processors. This could be supplemented by maracas and tambourines – and by occasional blasts from a trumpet. The feel should be celebratory and spontaneous rather than formal and regimented.

- Some participants could carry palms. Others could carry small placards or banners:
  - 'Jesus our King'
  - 'He made the blind to see'.

- Occasionally the procession breaks out into chanting:
  - *Procession leader: Blessed is he*
  - *Response: who comes in the name of the Lord.*
  - *(Repeat)*
  - *Leader: What's his name?*
  - *Response: Je–sus.*
  - *(Repeat)*

- The route and size of the procession are obviously dependent on architecture. However, the basic idea is that the procession completes a number of laps of the church.

- The running order is very simple (procession – observers' dialogue – congregational hymn – procession . . .) and is set out clearly in the text. It is based on the following assumptions:
  - During the observers' dialogue: the procession is stationary and silent.
  - While the congregation is singing: the procession is moving but silent.

    This means that there needs to be some form of pre-arranged signal (e.g. a particular sound from one of the instruments) so that members of the procession know when to stop and be silent in readiness for the observers' dialogue. These sorts of 'interactions' can be tricky. So, even though the basic format is a simple one, you might find it helpful to have a rehearsal for the observers and procession members.

- A picture on a screen depicting Jesus' entry into Jerusalem could be helpful. One can be found at <www.advent2harvest.co.uk>.

The observers

There are two observers. They can be either male or female.

In terms of location, they are not part of the procession itself.

Hymns

I have included suggestions for the three hymns that are used during the procession.

- 'Ride on, ride on in majesty' (verses 1, 2 and 5)
- 'All glory, laud and honour' (verses 1 and 5)
- 'My song is love unknown' (verses 3 and 1).

The first two of these fit well in the context of a procession. The third strikes a more thoughtful note once the procession has departed.

I have chosen these three hymns because their words provide particularly strong connections with the observers' dialogue. There are contemporary hymns with Palm Sunday themes but I have not identified any that offer such a good match with the text.

At some point in the service, the congregation will need to be briefed about their role.

A note about age

It is good to have a wide range of ages represented in the procession – from youngsters to the elderly – and it is important not to exclude those whose mobility is constrained (wheelchairs welcome!).

The 'Palm Sunday procession' text has not been written specifically for children. However, many children would enjoy being part of the procession and would contribute much to it.

Reflection

I have added a short reflection. Its use presupposes that palm crosses have been distributed to members of the congregation.

If appropriate, this could be used after 'My song is love unknown', or later on in the service.

It could also be used as a short stand-alone meditation for the beginning of Holy Week.

PALM SUNDAY PROCESSION

The picture showing Jesus' entry into Jerusalem comes up on the screen.

Silence

The sounds of the approaching procession can now just be heard.

The volume gradually increases and the procession comes into sight. The participants start to process around the church – they occasionally break out into chanting.

After an appropriate period of time (not too long), the procession stops moving and falls silent, except for the drums – their hushed rhythms can still, perhaps, just be heard.

Observer 1	What a crowd! There must be thousands here … thousands!
Observer 2	Look at those people over there … over there, beyond the well. They're cutting branches off the trees to make a carpet for him.
Observer 1	I don't think the city's seen anything like this since the Jerusalem Javelins won the grand final of the Chariot Racers Cup. What a victory parade that was. But this … this crowd is incredible!

Pause

Observer 2	So what do you think of him then … Jesus, I mean?
Observer 1	Well, he's certainly got a good turnout … and he's got some courage too. And from what I hear, he's a genuinely good guy. But it does make you wonder, doesn't it?
Observer 2	Wonder what … whether it's all going to end in tears?
Observer 1	Absolutely. Riding in here like that … and the crowd reacting … getting excited … proclaiming him as their king. I mean, it's not exactly the sort of scene to help the authorities sleep easily in their beds at night.
Observer 2	This city's smouldering at the best of times … with its military politics and its religious politics. It won't take much to set it alight.
Observer 1	Mind you, he is making the point that he's coming in peace … riding on a donkey. But even so, you can't help but think that he might be riding headlong into disaster.
Observer 2	I know what you're saying, but I've always had a sense that there's something a bit different about this man. When you consider all that we've heard about him, you just get the feeling that if there is trouble … I don't know quite how to put this … If there is trouble, it won't be by accident … it won't be because he's out of his depth.

Hymn: congregation seated; procession moving but silent.

> Ride on, ride on in majesty!
> Hark, all the tribes hosanna cry;
> thy humble beast pursues his road
> with palms and scattered garments strowed.

Ride on, ride on in majesty!
In lowly pomp ride on to die;
O Christ, thy triumphs now begin
o'er captive death and conquered sin.

Ride on, ride on in majesty!
In lowly pomp ride on to die;
bow thy meek head to mortal pain,
then take, O God, thy power, and reign.

After the congregation has finished singing, the procession continues with instruments playing and occasional chanting.

After an appropriate period of time, the procession stops moving and falls silent – except for the hushed beat of the drums.

Observer 1	Some people say he's the new David. Another great king sent by God …to free us from Roman rule and make us a great nation again.
Observer 2	Maybe, but from what I've heard about his teaching, picking a fight with the Romans doesn't seem to figure on his agenda. And as you said, he's chosen to enter the city on a donkey – that's a symbol of a king coming in peace …not of an armed uprising.
Observer 1	But people say that he's always preaching about the coming of God's kingdom.
Observer 2	I know. I've heard that as well. But I've also heard that a lot of this teaching is actually about how we should live our lives.
Observer 1	What do you mean …how we should live our lives?
Observer 2	All sorts of things … …prayer …that when we pray, we should think of God as a really good dad …and lots about how we should treat each other …in our everyday relationships … …and teaching about money …society …the importance of standing with the poor and the disadvantaged.
Observer 1	But what's that got to do with returning the nation to the Jewish people?
Observer 2	Perhaps it's a different sort of a kingdom.
Observer 1	A different sort of a kingdom?
Observer 2	Yes, perhaps he's not interested in ruling in a palace but in our hearts and minds.

Pause

Observer 1	Ehm …that's a bit different …

Pause

Observer 1	*(reflectively)* You mean a kingdom of love.

Hymn: congregation seated; procession moving but silent.

> *Chorus:*
> *All glory, laud and honour,*
> *to thee, Redeemer King,*
> *to whom the lips of children*
> *made sweet hosannas ring.*

> Thou art the king of Israel,
> thou David's royal Son,
> who in the Lord's name comest,
> the king and blessed one.
>
> Thou didst accept their praises,
> accept the prayers we bring,
> who in all good delightest,
> thou good and gracious king.

After the congregation has finished singing, the procession continues with instruments playing and occasional chanting.

After an appropriate period of time, the procession stops moving and falls silent – except for the hushed beat of the drums.

Observer 1   Well, if there aren't going to be any provocative gestures against the Romans then there'll be some people in the city who are going to be pretty disappointed.

Observer 2   Absolutely …

Pause

Observer 2   But why is he coming to Jerusalem now?

Observer 1   I suppose he wants to make his message better known in the big city … the centre … the hub.

Observer 2   And it is Passover at the end of the week.

Observer 1   But is he planning to do something … make some big religious statement … do something that makes a bit of an impact?

Observer 2   I don't know … I really don't know.

Observer 1   I wonder if anybody will still be talking about Jesus of Nazareth in 100 years' time.

Pause

Observer 2   You know, I rather think they might be.

Observer 1   Well, never mind 100 years, if these sorts of scenes carry on he'll be lucky to see the week out.

Pause

Observer 2   You certainly get the feeling. One way or another it's going to be one of those weeks.

The procession moves off for a final lap before moving out of sight. The volume gradually diminishes until all that can be heard are the barely audible rhythms of the drums and the occasional plaintive blasts of the trumpet. The procession then falls silent.

Silence

Hymn: congregation seated.

> Sometimes they strew his way,
> and his sweet praises sing;
> resounding all the day
> hosannas to their king;
> then 'Crucify!' is all their breath,
> and for his death they thirst and cry.

My song is love unknown,
my Saviour's love to me,
love to the loveless shown,
that they might lovely be.
O who am I, that for my sake,
my Lord should take frail flesh and die?

REFLECTION

Can I ask you to pick up your palm crosses?

The first thing we notice about a palm cross is, obviously, its shape.
It is a symbol of the cross on which Christ died,
a symbol of our forgiveness.

But consider also the weight of a palm cross ... consider its texture.
It is not an object of any great strength.
It is flimsy: easy to crumple, cut, shred, distort.
It speaks to us of vulnerability.
It speaks to us of how vulnerable Jesus must have felt as he entered Jerusalem on that first Palm Sunday, knowing what lay ahead of him during the coming week.

Pause

What, we wonder, made him feel most vulnerable:
the prospect of rejection and humiliation ... of physical pain, and dying ... of spiritual loneliness?
   Was it the crushing weight of responsibility? A fear that he might fail?

Pause

We have reflected on the vulnerabilities of Jesus.
   And, as we hold these frail crosses, we reflect, finally, just for a moment, on our own vulnerabilities
   ... on our hurts and fears ... and insecurities.

Pause

We conclude with some words from the Gospel of Matthew – words that refer to Jesus:

> A bent reed, he will not break;
> a flickering lamp, he will never put out.[2]

Silence

GOOD FRIDAY MEDITATION: TO THE FOOT OF THE CROSS

INTRODUCTION

'To the foot of the cross' offers a programme for a meditative Good Friday service. It consists of:

- Bible readings
- a series of short meditations on the crucifixion in the form of personal stories
- congregational hymns
- periods of silence
- music to listen to.

The material can be used selectively to produce a shorter programme.

The personal stories could be used in other contexts – and particularly in the more meditative forms of worship during Holy Week.

PREPARATION

The format is one that would benefit from a number of different voices.

Music

I have suggested that music (CD or download) is played during two of the periods of individual reflection. Possible selections:

- J. S. Bach, *St Matthew Passion* ('O Sacred Heart …')
- E. Morricone, 'The Mission (Gabriel's Oboe)': from the soundtrack of the film (Virgin, 1986)
- W. A. Mozart, 'Ave Verum Corpus'.

I have left the choice of hymns to local knowledge and custom.

Handouts

You might like to consider supporting the spoken word by producing a handout containing the text of the personal stories. If so, please see pages 2 and 45–7.

BACKGROUND THEOLOGICAL NOTES

What was happening on that first Good Friday?

Why was the cross necessary for our salvation?

Throughout the Church's history, there has always been intensive reflection on the meaning of the cross and, over the centuries, a number of theories of the atonement have emerged.[1] 'To the foot of the cross' explores particular aspects of the meaning of the crucifixion through the medium of four personal stories. While you can recognize elements of particular theories of the atonement within the stories, they have not been written to present these theories in a systematic way.

Finally, it needs to be emphasized that the different stories do not stand in competition with each other. They are intended to convey complementary insights. Perhaps the atonement is very much one of those areas of our faith where truth is found in allowing various perspectives and approaches to *rub shoulders with each other*[2] rather than in embracing one understanding exclusively.

TO THE FOOT OF THE CROSS

Opening hymn

PRAYER

Lord, it is not easy to grasp the enormity of this day.
We cannot plumb its depths.
We sometimes wonder why you died in this way.
We wonder why such a death was necessary for our salvation.
As we follow you now to the foot of the cross,
assist our understanding …
and open our hearts.
Amen.

BIBLE READING: INJUSTICE, MARK 15.6–15

Meditation

Reader 1 During this service, we are going to listen to four meditations about Jesus' death on the cross on that first Good Friday. Each of the meditations takes the form of a short personal story; and each story suggests a particular aspect of the meaning of the cross.
 This is the first story.

We do our best to be good parents. Of course, the kids misbehave sometimes. When this happens, we try to do two things. We try to make sure that, at some point, we reassure them ... that although what they've done is wrong, we still love them every bit as much. This usually involves a bit of a hug and a squeeze. But when their behaviour has been particularly bad, we do also punish them. For Lara – she's the younger one – this usually means that she has to go and sit on the stairs for a while. But Scott gets grounded. We have to do it. When they're doing things that are wrong. When they're doing things that are hurtful to other people. We don't want them growing up like that.

We feel that when we punish them, what we're trying to do is to emphasize how wrong something is. We're making a stand ... because we love them.

In a way, it's because of my experience of being a parent that I can understand why God takes human wrongdoing so seriously. I wouldn't want a God who didn't care about our selfishness and malice ... or about injustice and violence. I'd hate that. I'd feel let down.

For me, this is an important part of the meaning of Good Friday – of the crucifixion.

God couldn't just turn a blind eye to the ways in which we human beings can be so incredibly destructive. He couldn't just stand by and do nothing. He couldn't just leave us thinking that everything was okay when it wasn't okay. That wouldn't be love. That wouldn't be forgiving us ... that would be giving up on us ...

And sometimes words are not enough.

God had to *make a stand* ... just like parents do.

The difference is that God bore the cost of the punishment himself ... on the cross.

God demonstrated the terrible destructiveness of our dark side by allowing himself to be destroyed by it.

Short period of silence for reflection

Hymn

BIBLE READING: BULLYING AND MOCKERY, MARK 15.16–20

Meditation

Reader 2   This is the second story.

> I think that some people find it very hard to accept forgiveness. Perhaps we all find it hard … but some of us more than others. But if you haven't been able to accept that somebody has truly forgiven you then the relationship with that person will never feel right. There will always be a shadow hanging over it. The relationship will always be held back.
>
> Some of my own relationships have been rather complicated ones and perhaps it's because of this that I have always struggled when it comes to accepting forgiveness. But this is also why Good Friday is so important to me.
>
> I can look at the cross and know for an absolute certainty that God loves me and has forgiven me. I know that there are lots of different dimensions to what happened on that first Good Friday. But, for me, God is so generous. He knew that we needed something as tangible – as real – as the cross to hold on to.
>
> … to show us that there is nothing beyond the reach of his forgiveness.

Music

BIBLE READING: CRUCIFIXION, MARK 15.21–26

Meditation

Reader 3 Our next story takes the form of a parable. It points us to the way in which Jesus not only paid the price for our destructiveness but also initiated a healing process through which life and relationships could be restored.

So, this is the third story.

I was a bit of a bad lad when I was younger. There was a group of us. We always had our eyes open for an opportunity – housebreaking, car crime. Nothing big.

I remember once, we trashed this pensioner's flat … and all we took was his cash, a few quid, and two or three items that we knew we'd be able to sell on. We were pretty confident that we'd got away with it. But you always wondered whether the police were going to pay you a visit.

Then the next thing we knew, the old guy himself comes round. He said he knew that we'd broken into his flat. He certainly had guts turning up like that. But when he told us what he wanted to do, that really bowled us over.

He said that he'd provide all the tools, and pay the cost of all the materials, and work with us to put his place back to rights.

So we worked with him in his flat. None of us were what you would call skilled. But he was always chatting with us and showing us what to do. And, of course, I started to get to know him … and it felt good to be able to do something positive.

What a great bloke!

Changed my life, that did![3]

Short period of silence for reflection

Hymn

BIBLE READING: HUMILIATION, MARK 15.29–32A

Meditation

Reader 4   This is the final story.

When I was about 14, my friend and I walked out on to the beach of a large estuary. We then suddenly found ourselves cut off by the speed of the incoming tide. My friend was taller than me and managed to haul herself up on to a sort of jetty that had been built out into the water. But however hard I tried, I couldn't manage to climb up on to it. I'll never forget what she did next. She jumped back into the water to be with me. Eventually, we managed to wade through some thick mud to safety, but it was a close call.

As the years went by, that incident on the estuary, and my friend's actions, often seemed like a real-life parable to me.

Some people see God as distant. They see him as being remote – aloof, unfeeling, invulnerable – while, in contrast, we human beings struggle through life with our vulnerabilities and sufferings, frailties and insecurities.

But for me, God is not distant at all. God became one of us at Bethlehem. In his life and death, he shared fully in our vulnerabilities and our sufferings ... to the point of dying in such an unjust and awful way.

The cross shows me that there is no limit to how far God is willing to go to be one with us ... to identify with us ... to be part of us ... to share not only in our joys but in our anguish.

And I have faith that because God has entered so fully into human life then, ultimately, all will be well for us.

Music

BIBLE READING: DEATH, MARK 15.33–39

Short period of silence for reflection

Closing hymn

Blessing

FIRST STORY

We do our best to be good parents. Of course, the kids misbehave sometimes. When this happens, we try to do two things. We try to make sure that, at some point, we reassure them ... that although what they've done is wrong, we still love them every bit as much. This usually involves a bit of a hug and a squeeze. But when their behaviour has been particularly bad, we do also punish them. For Lara – she's the younger one – this usually means that she has to go and sit on the stairs for a while. But Scott gets grounded. We have to do it. When they're doing things that are wrong. When they're doing things that are hurtful to other people. We don't want them growing up like that.

We feel that when we punish them, what we're trying to do is to emphasize how wrong something is. We're making a stand ... because we love them.

In a way, it's because of my experience of being a parent that I can understand why God takes human wrongdoing so seriously. I wouldn't want a God who didn't care about our selfishness and malice ... or about injustice and violence. I'd hate that. I'd feel let down.

For me, this is an important part of the meaning of Good Friday – of the crucifixion.

God couldn't just turn a blind eye to the ways in which we human beings can be so incredibly destructive. He couldn't just stand by and do nothing. He couldn't just leave us thinking that everything was okay when it wasn't okay. That wouldn't be love. That wouldn't be forgiving us ... that would be giving up on us ...

And sometimes words are not enough.

God had to *make a stand* ... just like parents do.

The difference is that God bore the cost of the punishment himself ... on the cross.

God demonstrated the terrible destructiveness of our dark side by allowing himself to be destroyed by it.

SECOND STORY

I think that some people find it very hard to accept forgiveness. Perhaps we all find it hard …but some of us more than others. But if you haven't been able to accept that somebody has truly forgiven you then the relationship with that person will never feel right. There will always be a shadow hanging over it. The relationship will always be held back.

Some of my own relationships have been rather complicated ones and perhaps it's because of this that I have always struggled when it comes to accepting forgiveness. But this is also why Good Friday is so important to me.

I can look at the cross and know for an absolute certainty that God loves me and has forgiven me. I know that there are lots of different dimensions to what happened on that first Good Friday. But, for me, God is so generous. He knew that we needed something as tangible – as real – as the cross to hold on to.

…to show us that there is nothing beyond the reach of his forgiveness.

THIRD STORY

I was a bit of a bad lad when I was younger. There was a group of us. We always had our eyes open for an opportunity – housebreaking, car crime. Nothing big.

I remember once, we trashed this pensioner's flat …and all we took was his cash, a few quid, and two or three items that we knew we'd be able to sell on. We were pretty confident that we'd got away with it. But you always wondered whether the police were going to pay you a visit.

Then the next thing we knew, the old guy himself comes round. He said he knew that we'd broken into his flat. He certainly had guts turning up like that. But when he told us what he wanted to do, that really bowled us over.

He said that he'd provide all the tools, and pay the cost of all the materials, and work with us to put his place back to rights.

So we worked with him in his flat. None of us were what you would call skilled. But he was always chatting with us and showing us what to do. And, of course, I started to get to know him …and it felt good to be able to do something positive.

What a great bloke!

Changed my life, that did!

FINAL STORY

When I was about 14, my friend and I walked out on to the beach of a large estuary. We then suddenly found ourselves cut off by the speed of the incoming tide. My friend was taller than me and managed to haul herself up on to a sort of jetty that had been built out into the water. But however hard I tried, I couldn't manage to climb up on to it. I'll never forget what she did next. She jumped back into the water to be with me. Eventually, we managed to wade through some thick mud to safety, but it was a close call.

As the years went by, that incident on the estuary, and my friend's actions, often seemed like a real-life parable to me.

Some people see God as distant. They see him as being remote – aloof, unfeeling, invulnerable – while, in contrast, we human beings struggle through life with our vulnerabilities and sufferings, frailties and insecurities.

But for me, God is not distant at all. God became one of us at Bethlehem. In his life and death, he shared fully in our vulnerabilities and our sufferings ... to the point of dying in such an unjust and awful way.

The cross shows me that there is no limit to how far God is willing to go to be one with us ... to identify with us ... to be part of us ... to share not only in our joys but in our anguish.

And I have faith that because God has entered so fully into human life then, ultimately, all will be well for us.

EASTER DAY VIGIL: HE IS RISEN!

INTRODUCTION

'He is risen!' is a short order of service for a vigil early in the morning on Easter Day.

The dramatic character of the service derives from the way in which a combination of candles and electric lighting is used to achieve a gradual increase of light within the church building: from total darkness to full light. This practice, which may already be familiar to you, is intended to symbolize light overcoming darkness and the dawning realization of the first disciples that Jesus had indeed risen . . . he was alive.

The vigil can stand alone or serve as a prelude to a celebration of Holy Communion.

You might also like to consider the possibility of having breakfast together after the service.

PREPARATION

Timing

Given that Easter is a moveable feast, this needs to be determined with some care. It is important that the service commences in darkness.

Lighting

There are obviously different ways to achieve a gradual build-up of light in a building and you will need to find the one that is most appropriate for your architecture. The method outlined below entails the use of a number of candles, including

- a large (paschal) candle situated at the front of the church
- a sufficient number of small candles (in appropriate holders) to give one to each member of the congregation.

One of the foremost practical considerations with a service of this form concerns the availability of sufficient light for people to be able to use hymnbooks and/or service sheets. In the order set out below, it is envisaged that members of the congregation will use handheld candles for a period of time to enable them to do this. However, holding small lighted candles in cardboard holders can become uncomfortable pretty quickly. Thus I have endeavoured to keep this phase of the service relatively brief.

Given the use of handheld candles, a safety notice will need to be given prior to the service, and the usual precautions taken.

Readings

The Bible readings are from the Good News Bible. They have been slightly adapted to fit the context.

The format is one that would benefit from a number of different voices.

Music

In choosing hymns, you might like to consider matching the gradual increase of light with a corresponding development in the vigour of the music – for example, moving from 'Now the green blade riseth' through 'Led like a lamb to the slaughter' to one of the most rousing of the Easter hymns or modern worship songs.

HE IS RISEN!

The lights in the church are turned off.

A short period of silence follows.

There is the sound of a door opening.

A solitary lit candle is brought into the back of the church.

An announcement is read from the back of the church using the light of the candle.

> He who is the source of light . . .
> He who is the source of life . . .
> He who is the prince of peace . . .
> He who is the creator of love . . .
> He is not dead.
> He is risen . . . he is alive.

The solitary candle is now brought slowly forward to the front of the church. It is used to light the large paschal candle.

Bible reading

John 20.1–8

Early on Sunday morning, while it was still dark, Mary Magdalene went to the tomb and saw that the stone had been taken away from the entrance. She went running to Simon Peter and the other disciple, whom Jesus loved, and told them, 'They have taken the Lord from the tomb, and we don't know where they have put him!'

Then Peter and the other disciple went to the tomb. The two of them were running, but the other disciple ran faster than Peter and reached the tomb first. He bent over and saw the linen wrappings, but he did not go in.

Behind him came Simon Peter, and he went straight into the tomb. He saw the linen wrappings lying there and the cloth which had been round Jesus' head. It was not lying with the linen wrappings but was rolled up by itself. Then the other disciple, who had reached the tomb first, also went in. He saw and believed.

> He who bore our frailties and our flaws on the cross . . .
> He who picks up the fallen . . .
> He who will never put out a flickering lamp or break a bent reed . . .
> He who is the defender of the poor . . .
> He who is our friend, and our confidant . . .
> He is not dead.
> He is risen . . . he is alive.

The light from the paschal candle is now 'taken' to each of the worshippers and used to light their individual candles.

Hymn

At the conclusion of the hymn, the electric lighting in the sanctuary (or comparable area) is turned on.

Bible reading

John 20.11–16

Mary stood crying outside the tomb. While she was still crying, she bent over and looked in the tomb and saw two angels there dressed in white, sitting where the body of Jesus had been, one at the head and the other at the feet. 'Woman, why are you crying?' they asked her.

She answered, 'They have taken my Lord away, and I do not know where they have put him!'

Then she turned round and saw Jesus standing there; but she did not know that it was Jesus. 'Woman, why are you crying?' Jesus asked her. 'Who is it that you are looking for?'

Mary thought he was the gardener, so she said to him, 'If you took him away, sir, tell me where you have put him, and I will go and get him.'

Jesus said to her, 'Mary!'

She turned towards him and ... said, 'Teacher!'

> He who is *our* teacher ...
> He who is our inspiration and our vision ...
> He whose call gives purpose to our lives ...
>
> He is not dead.

All   **He is risen, he is alive.**

All the electric lighting is now turned on.

(Members of the congregation will probably be more comfortable if they extinguish their handheld candles at this point.)

Hymn

Bible reading

John 20.19–22 and 26–28

It was late that Sunday evening, and the disciples were gathered together behind locked doors, because they were afraid of the Jewish authorities. Then Jesus came and stood among them. 'Peace be with you,' he said. After saying this, he showed them his hands and his side. The disciples were filled with joy at seeing the Lord.

Jesus said to them again, 'Peace be with you. As the Father sent me, so I send you.' Then he breathed on them and said, 'Receive the Holy Spirit' ...

[Thomas was not with the other disciples when Jesus appeared to them and he would not believe.]

A week later, the disciples were together again ... and Thomas was with them. The doors were locked, but Jesus came and stood among them and said, 'Peace be with you.' Then he said to Thomas, 'Look at my hands, touch the scars; stretch out your hand and put it in my side. Stop your doubting, and believe.'

Thomas answered him, 'My Lord and my God.'

> He who is God in the midst of us …
> He who is our hero …
> He who battles against all that violates human dignity and spoils human life …
> He who is the death of death …
> He who is our forgiveness and our hope …
> He is not dead.

All　　**He is risen, he is alive.**

Hymn

The vigil concludes with the sharing of the peace.

> After Jesus had risen from the dead, he came and stood among his followers and said to them,
>> 'Peace be with you.'

> The peace of the Lord be always with you.

All　　**And also with you.**

> We share the peace of Christ with one another.

PENTECOST: THE SPIRIT OF JESUS

INTRODUCTION

'The Spirit of Jesus' can be used as a short meditation or reflective sermon.

This item focuses on the work of the Holy Spirit in moral and social renewal.

PREPARATION

Readings

It would probably be helpful to have two or three readers.

Music

I have made provision for the inclusion of two periods of personal reflection. You might like to provide music during these times.

Suggestions:

- 'O thou who camest from above' (music only, organ)

- Vivaldi, *The Four Seasons*, 'Spring', Allegro.

Simultaneous text

You might like to consider supporting the *spoken word* by displaying the text on a screen as it is read. If so, please see the introductory section ('Simultaneous text') on page 1.

PENTECOST: THE SPIRIT OF JESUS

READING 1

First voice   We start with two sentences about the Holy Spirit from the New Testament.

God has poured out his love into our hearts by means of the Holy Spirit, who is God's gift to us.[1]

The Spirit produces love, joy, peace, patience, kindness, goodness, faithfulness, humility, and self-control.[2]

At the very heart of the Christian faith is the belief that the Spirit of Jesus, the Holy Spirit, is still in the world today
…to inspire us
…to strengthen us.

Brief pause/change of voice

Jesus' life was one of compassion.
He picked up the fallen.
He reached out selflessly to those in need.
His Spirit of compassion is still in the world today
…and can dwell in us.

Change of voice   Jesus lived for the whole of humanity.
He cut through social barriers.
He cut through divisions of politics, religion and race.
His Spirit of humanity is still in the world today
…and can inspire us.

Change of voice   Jesus' life was one of courage.
He was never dominated by the pressure to conform.
He stood up to the bullies and a heartless establishment.
His Spirit of courage is still in the world today
…and can fortify us.

Change of voice   Jesus' life was one of forgiveness.
He even forgave those who drove nails through his hands.
His Spirit of forgiveness is still in the world today
…and can empower us.

Brief pause/change of voice

God has sent to us the Spirit of Jesus.
And when we respond to the Spirit's promptings
…then the Spirit strengthens us.

God has sent to us the Spirit of Jesus
to empower us to play our part in healing the world's wounds and mending its divisions.

Pause for thought (music)

READING 2

First voice The Spirit of Jesus,
the Spirit of Love,
perhaps most often works through people in ways that are little noticed:

Quiet acts of forgiveness and reconciliation ... and of peacemaking ...
non-pretentious acts of support and kindness ... of attentiveness and protection ...
timely words of hope ...
conscientiousness well beyond the call of duty ...
integrity under pressure.

But offerings such as these,
an almost infinite number of them given each day,
ripple out across the creation ...
healing ...
restoring ...
preserving ...
sustaining.

Change of voice At the other end of the scale,
the Spirit's work is sometimes writ large in human history.
It is witnessed, for example, in the immense contribution that Christ-inspired men and
women have made to social reform ...
to the advancement of medicine and the development of health care ...
to the advancement of education ...
to movements for peace and for economic and political change.

Brief pause

The Spirit of Jesus works through the followers of Jesus;
but the Spirit is not confined to working through the Church and its members.[3]
And as Christians, we should not be possessive about these matters.
Indeed, when we pray,
for our communities, for our society, for the world in its needs,
we declare our belief that the Spirit blows across the whole of creation.
The Spirit blows where he will ...
never coercing ... but prompting ... and sustaining.

Pause for thought (music)

CONCLUDING PRAYER

Lord Jesus, may we who confess your name
…we who draw our identity from being your followers,
be ever open to your Spirit of Love.
And, wherever we see peace and restoration in the world,
may we give glory to God in the highest.
Amen.

HARVEST: A TWENTY-FIRST-CENTURY CELEBRATION OF THE CREATOR, CREATION AND CREATIVITY

INTRODUCTION

'Harvest: A twenty-first-century celebration' brings together

- reflective readings

- music

- the construction of a colourful and dramatic harvest montage.

The material can be used in a variety of settings. It could provide the central core of a stand-alone service or it could fit within liturgical contexts as an extended ministry of the word.

This is an item with many options and possibilities that could be developed. But equally, as I shall indicate later on, you could use it to create something really quite simple.

PREPARATION

Reflective readings

The text consists of a number of readings. If you are under particular time constraints, you will find some scope to use these selectively. Readings 1, 2, 3 and 5 could be regarded as a core text.

It would probably be helpful to use more than one reader.

The construction of the harvest montage takes place during Reading 5.

You might like to consider supporting the *spoken word* by displaying the text on a screen as it is read. If so, please see the introductory section ('Simultaneous text') on page 1.

Music

The basic concept is that the readings are interspersed with music – congregational hymns, choir anthems, instrumental pieces (organ, music group, CD, download . . .). Harvest time offers a wonderful range of possibilities for inspirational music – traditional and contemporary, classical and popular. I have made one or two further practical suggestions within the text.

The harvest montage

A key part of the celebration is the construction of the montage.

At designated points during the readings, a variety of items – from food and drink to fabrics and ceramics, from hi-tech electronic equipment to books and building materials – are brought forward to the front of the church. The items are then gradually arranged to form a large and colourful montage. The intention is to provide a striking visual interpretation of the rich and varied potential of God's creation – of the almost limitless array of possibilities and opportunities that it offers – and of human creativity and ingenuity.

As has already been indicated, the montage is constructed during Reading 5. It needs to be planned in some detail beforehand. The items that form the montage need to be selected carefully so as to stimulate members of the congregation to reflect upon the awesome character of the creation and the immense width of resources it provides. The montage also needs to be designed both for maximum visual and aesthetic impact (the medium is the message) and for ease of construction.

The lists below provide a selection of the sorts of items that could be included in the montage. The Reader's words are extracts from Reading 5.

There is inevitably a degree of overlap between the different sections.

While it is suggested that traditional harvest produce is brought up first, the fabrics can be used to make an attractive backdrop for the montage as a whole.

Reader   So the people of the earth brought forth a harvest:
a harvest of nutrition and taste;

Appropriate items are brought forward: bread, fresh food, processed food, bottled drinks, tap water ...

They are arranged in position.

Reader   a harvest of design and image, colour and shape;

Appropriate items are brought forward and arranged in position. These could include: colourful textiles and fabrics (coverings, drapes, items of clothing), a small piece of furniture, a painting or photograph, flowers, ceramics, jewellery, embroidery ...

Reader   a harvest of discovery and knowledge, medicine and engineering, transport and communications;

Items here could include: a wheel from a car (rolled down the aisle), medicines, a laptop computer, tools (both from a previous age and contemporary power tools: drill, vacuum cleaner, hairdryer), a bucket of coal, house bricks, electrical wiring, a section of pipe, a pair of spectacles ...

Reader   a harvest of interpretation and reflection, mood and music;

Possible items: a varied selection of books (fiction, non-fiction), local and national newspapers, magazines, a musical instrument, a picture of Captain Mainwaring of *Dad's Army* (see below), a varied selection of CDs and DVDs, a painting, photograph or sculpture ...

Reader   And as people developed particular aspects of the potential within themselves
– to relate, co-operate, care, nurture –
they brought forth the fruits of community.

Examples: a policeman's helmet, a judge's wig, a nurse's hat, a fireman's helmet, a ballot box, a lollipop (as used at a school crossing), sports equipment, a football jersey, toys, a scout uniform, a pint of beer, a disability (mobility) scooter...

The montage could also incorporate a rolling screen displaying further examples of ways in which humanity has harnessed the potential of God's creation. Possible ideas here could include: the *Rocket* steam locomotive, Eurostar, sea defences, irrigation systems, a science laboratory, the Hadron Collider, the UN building in New York, alphabets, examples of working communities (school, building site, office, nursing home...), shops, a bank, CAB, a counselling room, a farmworker looking after animals, a garden, a film star, a museum, the Gherkin, direction boards showing the different departments or units in a hospital, an industrial estate or a university, a fishing boat or freighter...

Use of a rolling screen would preclude the use of simultaneous text in Reading 5.

I think it is important that a montage includes both contemporary and historic items or images (as the saying reminds us, we sit on giants' shoulders); and that it includes global references as well as local flavour.

An expectant mood can be created if the items are brought up to some appropriate music.

Suggestions:

- 'Albatross', Fleetwood Mac
- 'Green onions', Booker T. and the M.G.s
- Water Music, G. F. Handel.

There is also scope to inject elements of surprise and humour: a disability (mobility) scooter – with somebody on it; the person holding a picture of Captain Mainwaring could say, 'Don't tell him, Pike'...

The montage can also be managed in a very simple way. A rolling screen is not essential! In one church that used 'Harvest: A twenty-first-century celebration', those responsible for the service simply placed a large table at the top of the chancel steps and a varied, but carefully thought out, selection of items were brought forward and placed on it.

BACKGROUND THEOLOGICAL NOTES

The reflective readings take their rise from the first of the creation stories at the beginning of the book of Genesis. There we read that God made human beings in his own image so that they could exercise dominion over the rest of the created order.[1] The narrative conveys a sense of empowerment: human beings are made in God's image in order to equip them to exercise dominion. The narrative also incorporates a sense of calling: God invites those who bear his image to fulfil this role. Within Jewish and Christian traditions, 'dominion' is not interpreted as autonomous rule. Rather, it is understood that humankind is called to a responsible and caring stewardship of the planet and its varied resources. Indeed, the Old Testament commentator Gerhard von Rad holds that the concept of dominion in Genesis is best interpreted in terms of vice-regency. God reigns supreme over all and calls humanity to serve as his vice-regent on the earth.[2]

Finally, we may note that the calling to dominion belongs to the human race as a whole. It is given in creation. It is part of human identity. It is a vocation that exists – in its most fundamental and implicit form – in that deep and characteristic urge of human beings to develop their own capacities and shape the world.

HARVEST: A TWENTY-FIRST-CENTURY CELEBRATION OF THE CREATOR, CREATION AND CREATIVITY

INTRODUCTORY READINGS

God makes human beings in his own image so that they can fulfil a unique role in the creation.

Then God said, 'Let us make human beings in our image, after our likeness, to have dominion over the fish in the sea, the birds of the air, the cattle, all wild animals on land, and everything that creeps on the earth.' God created human beings in his own image; in the image of God he created them; male and female he created them. God blessed them and said to them, 'Be fruitful and increase, fill the earth and subdue it.'   (Genesis 1.26–28, REB)

When I look up at the heavens, the work of your fingers, the moon and stars which you arranged, what are human beings that you should be mindful of them, mere mortals that you should care about them? Yet you have made them little less than the gods. You have crowned their heads with glory and honour. You have given them dominion over all you have made.
                    (Psalm 8.3–6, REB, adapted)

From the beginning you have created all things and all your works echo the silent music of your praise. In the fullness of time you made us in your image, the crown of all creation.
                    (From the Church of England's services for Holy Communion, Eucharistic Prayer G)

Musical interlude: congregational hymn

READING 1

At that point,
planet earth was but a spinning mass in the vastness of space and time.
There was no life in its waters.
And on the dry lands,
there were no eyes to see the endless bare and barren rockscapes
– desolate places whose time had not yet come.

When the time did come,
life on God's earth had wondrous capacities:
to adapt, develop, evolve, diversify . . .
to self-repair, self-organize.

But this was only a start.
There was the possibility of so much more.
The creation was still brimming with potential
which in some way,
through some means,
needed to be drawn out.

So, when the next time was right,
God invited humankind to be his partner in his great creative work.

He called us to develop the immense potential of the earth.
He called us to develop the immense potential within ourselves.

The call was deep within us.

God did not just want us to play a minor role in the work of creation.
He wanted us to use our own ideas
. . . our own creativity
so that we could play our full part in shaping what the world was to become.

Musical interlude

READING 2

God wanted humankind to care for the world ... and to develop it.
In order that the people of the earth could be his partners in the work of creation,
in shaping what the world was to become,
God had bestowed upon them a unique potential.
The people of the earth bore God's image.

And, over time,
the members of the human race developed their unique potential
... and their distinctive way of life.

They demonstrated an intellectual curiosity and creativity that
discovered fire,
invented the wheel,
uncovered the secret of seeds – and used them ... and improved them.

They displayed an ability to generate and refine language –
to express complex thoughts and strong feelings,
to share plans and dreams,
to work co-operatively,
to pass accumulated knowledge down the generations.

They developed great skills and techniques –
to work with wood and stone, cloth and colour,
to create gardens and organize farms,
to bake, build, weld ...
to construct and operate machines.

They became wonderfully adept at discerning the earth's brimming potential.
They came to perceive an almost limitless array of possibilities in the world around them.
They discerned the potential
for medicine in flowers,
for metal in shale,
for locomotion in steam,
for electronics in silicon.

They unlocked the atom and probed stars.

Musical interlude

READING 3

Thus, over time,
we, the members of the human race,
developed our particular aptitudes –
for language,
for accumulating knowledge,
for acquiring skills.

We showed a capacity for a depth of emotional life,
and for a breadth of vision – social, moral, spiritual …

We showed the ability to develop great systems of social organization and economic
co-operation
– sometimes traversing continents and stretching across oceans.

We displayed the sort of … experimental imagination
that persisted in forcing air down a tube,
or scraping gut on gut,
until what came forth was music
… music to stir the depths of heart and soul.

And we exhibited an inclination to make relatively ordinary things
do extraordinary things:
to use liquidity,
oil, paste, pigment,
to express form, light, mood, meaning …

These are qualities and capabilities far, far beyond those possessed by any other creatures.
There is a distinctiveness about humanity.
Intellectually, emotionally, socially, artistically – we stand apart.
In respect of our moral and spiritual awareness – we stand apart.
There are no other species like us.
None that even come close to us.
To the eye of faith,
our distinctiveness reflects a unique endowment in creation
– the very image of God within us,
our capacity to shape the world.[3]

Musical interlude

READING 4

God did not only value people for their role in developing the creation.
He did not only value people for their aptitudes and abilities ... for their function.

God placed an eternal value on the life of each individual.
He enriched human life with a capacity for awe and wonder.
And God wanted the creatures who bore his image to understand,
and to enjoy,
the particular affection and kinship that he felt towards them.

And there was a generosity in God's dream for human life.
He fashioned us in such a way that we would be able to experience deep happiness in
being his partners in creation.
He created us such that we could find joy and fulfilment
in serving one another,
in developing our talents,
and in harnessing the rich potential of the earth.

Pause

READING 5

The construction of the harvest montage takes place during this reading. See the notes in the introduction to this chapter.

So the people of the earth brought forth a harvest:
a harvest of nutrition and taste;
a harvest of design and image, colour and shape;
a harvest of discovery and knowledge, medicine and engineering, transport and communications;
a harvest of interpretation and reflection, mood and music.
And as people developed particular aspects of the potential within themselves
– to relate, co-operate, care, nurture –
they brought forth the fruits of community.

Musical interlude: congregational hymn

A FORM OF CONFESSION

Minister   Lord, we,
the bearers of your image,
the crown of your creation,
confess that we have often abused the freedom that you have given to us.
We have destroyed as well as created.
We have brought forth ugliness as well as beauty.

Lord, forgive us,
for our failure to distribute the fruits of the earth with justice;
for the aggressive materialism that threatens to degrade the earth;
for the shallow consumerism that subverts our own creativity and dignity;
for the times when our attitude to possessions has been driven by greed or status.

Lord, forgive us.

All   **Lord, have mercy.**

Minister   Lord, forgive us,
for the times
when we have turned away from using words
to encourage and co-operate, to inspire and educate,
and have used them instead to
gossip and deceive, wound and belittle.

Lord, forgive us.

All   **Lord, have mercy.**

Minister   Lord, forgive us,
for the times
when we have turned away from using our ingenuity and resources
to feed and heal, protect and nurture,
and have used them instead
to devise means of exploitation and domination,
aggression and death.

Lord, forgive us.

All   **Lord, have mercy.**

Concluding prayer

Minister   Lord, your Son, Jesus Christ,
gave his life for our forgiveness.
Through him, you renewed your call for us to be your partners in the world.
May we live each day,
in every way,
as befits those who are bearers of your image.
Amen.

AN ALTERNATIVE CONCLUSION

But we,
the bearers of God's image,
the crown of his creation,
often abused the freedom that he had given to us.
We brought forth a mixed harvest.
We destroyed as well as created.
We brought forth ugliness as well as beauty.
Our unique abilities were put to good uses … and to terrible uses.
There were times when there seemed to be no limit to our destructiveness.
Sometimes we created hells on earth
… in war zones and on refugee trails
… among the fearful and the humiliated
… among the bullied and the starved.

Sometimes the earth groaned beneath the weight of pain that we created.

And some people of faith cried out to their God:
Why did you give us so much freedom?
The burden of it is too heavy.

Pause

So God became one of us.
In Jesus, he lived among us.

He showed us a better way to live.

And although we had violated his creation,
and had proudly placed ourselves at the centre of the universe as if we owned it;
and although we had been the cause of so much suffering and pain,
God opened wide his arms for us on the cross.
It was the most powerful embrace of human history.
We can still feel its warmth and certainty today.
It was an embrace that proclaimed God's love and forgiveness;
and in which his call for us to be his partners in creation was renewed.

Concluding prayer

We have celebrated the awesome character of God's creation.

We have also celebrated human skill and knowledge, initiative and imagination:
they are essential for the life of the creation.
They are essential … but without love and justice, they are not enough.

Lord, through creation, you have provided humanity with plenteous skills.
Through your risen conquering Son, you offer us the Spirit of Love.
May we each day embrace both
the way of love
and the particular skills that you have given to us.
So may we be your partners in the world
and help to bring in a good harvest.
Amen.

REMEMBRANCE SUNDAY: LORD, ARE YOU TEMPTED TO INTERVENE?

INTRODUCTION

This item is made up of a 'dramatic' reading, 'Lord, are you tempted to intervene?', and prayers. It works best if the prayers follow on directly after the reading.

LORD, ARE YOU TEMPTED TO INTERVENE?

Lord, are you sometimes tempted to intervene?
When the bullies are circling their prey in the playground – enjoying the fear in their victim's eyes:
are you tempted to intervene?

When the lie is on the lips;
when the gossip is gangrenous on the tongue;
when the predator's hand reaches to caress the knee:
are you tempted to intervene?

When we are arrogant in the face of injustice,
or apathetic in the face of poverty:
are you tempted to intervene?

When slave traders were about to embark on their brutal carnage;
when the clock was ticking down
to Passchendaele,
or Auschwitz;
when the dawn was breaking on the day of
Hiroshima,
or 9/11,
were you then,
on the verge of such unspeakable horrors,
tempted to intervene … to overrule … to put an end to it?

Lord, are you torn apart?
Does the heart within you that breaks with such suffering
tear against
the love within you that has created us free?

The truth is, of course, that we do not know all your ways.
We do know, however, that if you intervened when we were about to hurt each other,
then our freedom would be an illusion.
We would not be people.
We would be toys.

PRAYERS

Amid the agonies and the despair of war,
many have cried out:
Where is God now?
Why doesn't he intervene?
Why doesn't he do something?
And yet, Lord, in a different sense,
…in the most profound sense of all,
you have intervened.
Jesus lived among us.
He taught us a better way to live.
He showed us a better way to live.
His Spirit is still with us.
Help us to follow him,
and in so doing, find those paths that lead to the good of all.
This we ask in his name.
Amen.

Lord, we thank you for those men and women who have given so much
…when duty has been dangerous
…when aggression and violence have had to be stopped
…when wrongs have had to be righted.
Particularly today, we thank you for the courage and conscientiousness shown
    by members of the armed services…
and we give you our thanks for all those who have made the ultimate sacrifice.

Brief pause

Lord, we commit to you now, all those who are, in any way, the victims of war.

Brief pause

Lord, may they be
understood…
loved…
and renewed.
This we ask in Jesus' name,
Amen.

Heavenly Father, we lament
the aggressive self-interest,
the selective memories
and the short-sightedness
that can lead to war.
Yet we confess that we sometimes find these same faults and failings within our own lives.
So, as we pray today for peace in the world,
we ask that it may begin in us.[1]
This we ask in the name of Jesus,
the prince of peace.
Amen.

Heavenly Father,
we commit to you all those throughout the world who work for peace.
Give them wisdom for the complex tasks that they face.
Give them stamina, powers of perseverance, the ability to keep going
…and save them from disillusionment when the obstacles to peace
    seem insurmountable.
Heavenly Father,
we commit to you too, all those who work for justice.
Sustain and strengthen them in their endeavours;
and help us to always remember that without justice there can be no true peace.
In the name of Jesus, we pray.
Amen.

Part 2

OTHER MATERIAL

UPSIDE-DOWN PEOPLE, DRAMA 1: MATERIAL POSSESSIONS AND HAPPINESS

INTRODUCTION

This is the first of two dramas that look at the ways in which the teachings of Jesus turn many familiar values and attitudes upside down.

The second drama explores issues of reconciliation and peace.

PREPARATION

In both dramas, the setting is a room in a university. A screen, a laptop computer, a digital projector (all of which will be used in the dramas), piles of books and an academic gown should suffice to set the scene. Both items take the form of an interview between a television reporter and a university professor.

While the format here is a very straightforward one, the individuals who play the key roles do need to draw out the meaning of the text.

POWERPOINT

The dramas make use of a PowerPoint presentation. To download the fully prepared presentation, please go to <www.advent2harvest.co.uk> (see page 1 above). The contents for both dramas are as follows:

- slides (images) 1, 12: opening titles
- slides 10, 16: closing titles
- slides 2, 9, 13: Upside-down graphics
- other slides: these display short portions of text.

The locations are indicated clearly in the script below.

Biblical sources

For the sources of the sayings of Jesus, please see the note.[1]

Music

'O Lord, all the world belongs to you' would be a particularly appropriate choice of hymn.

You might like to find an appropriate piece of music to serve as a theme tune for the programme.

Suggestion: Vangelis, 'To the unknown man' (SME, 1977).

UPSIDE-DOWN PEOPLE, DRAMA I: MATERIAL POSSESSIONS AND HAPPINESS

Image 1 is displayed on the screen.

The programme's theme tune is played as the professor and the reporter take up their positions.

Reporter   Good evening and welcome to this edition of *The Way We Are Tonight*.
I'm here in the city of Comberford and I have with me one of the professors from the city's prestigious university.
Professor Jones, welcome to the programme.

Professor   Thank you. It's good to be with you.

Reporter   Professor Jones works in the areas of sociology and anthropology. He has recently made an extended study of the so-called 'Upside-down people'.
Professor, could you tell us something about these people?

Image 2

Professor   Well, they're people who have decided that it's best to live upside down. Some of my colleagues jokingly call them *Homo sapiens upsidedownus* or *Homo sapiens invertus*.

Reporter   Decided that it's best to live upside down. What does that mean exactly?

Professor   Well, Upside-downism has often had the feeling of a protest movement. One of its twentieth-century leaders called it counter-culture.[2] Its basic contention is that we, as human beings, need to turn many of our most common assumptions, many of our received wisdoms, upside down (*motions with arm*) – through 180 degrees, on their heads – if we are to make genuine progress.

Reporter   What sort of things are we talking about here, Professor?

Professor   It may help to go back to one of the most influential teachers of Upside-downism. Many of the most important Upside-down principles derive from Jesus of Nazareth who, as you know, lived around 2,000 years ago and developed a whole body of radical moral teaching –

Reporter (*interrupting*)   So, you mean Upside-downers are Christians ... churchgoers?

Professor   I wouldn't say it's quite that straightforward. Many Christians are upside down. But through the centuries, Christians – and churches – have not always adopted the principles of Upside-downism. On the other hand, there have been people outside of the Church – people of other faiths, people of no faith – who have been attracted by aspects of Upside-downism and sought to put them into practice.

Reporter   Okay, let's cut to the chase here, Professor. What sort of teachings are we talking about?

Professor   Well, as I said, many of the primary Upside-down teachings derive from Jesus of Nazareth and I've got a small selection of his sayings here.

Image 3

Professor   Here's the first one. Jesus was a very lively teacher. He could be quite provocative. His sayings – nowadays we would probably call some of them sound bites – were designed to get people thinking about their lives.

The professor reads Image 3.

Professor If we focus all our energies on self-advancement – or on protecting ourselves – then we will ultimately lose ourselves.

Image 4 is displayed and is read by the reporter.

Reporter Love your enemies instead of hating them.
Don't retaliate or try to get even when people maltreat you. Rather, forgive them … and keep forgiving them.
If somebody slaps you on the right cheek, let him slap your left cheek too.

Professor And I've two more.

Image 5 is displayed and read by the professor.

Professor Material possessions do not create lasting happiness.
More happiness comes from giving out than from getting something for yourself.

Image 6 is displayed and read by the reporter.

Reporter Whoever wants to be first among you, must be the servant of all.
The true meaning of power is being a slave.
Power is an opportunity – not for ego or control or wealth – but for self-sacrifice in the service of others.

Reporter (continues) Okay … I guess most of us can see one or two glimmers of truth in some of these sayings. But most people would say that a lot of this is rather naive … and some of it, frankly, a recipe for getting hurt.

Professor Possibly. But living according to our ideals often makes us vulnerable. That's just a fact of life. And Upside-down people would also say that we need to draw out the inner meaning of some of these sayings.

Reporter Can you give us an example of that, Professor?

Professor Well, take the issue of happiness and possessions.

Image 7

Professor (continues) Upside-downers are not advocating the hard grind of poverty. Indeed, they are usually in the forefront of those fighting against poverty and economic injustice.
And Christian Upside-downers have strong views about the importance of the creation … believing that God wants us to both care for the world and enjoy it.

Reporter So what are they concerned about?

Professor One of their fundamental contentions is that striving for ever more and more possessions – and getting ever more and more possessions – doesn't actually lead to people experiencing a depth of fulfilment in their lives … and is often a dangerous distraction from finding a deeper happiness.

Reporter So … if we think about people who embrace Upside-downism – in some form – what sort of things do they believe make for a deeper happiness?

Professor Okay, I've got something else that I can get up on the screen for you …
Here it is …

Image 8 is displayed and read by the professor.

Professor   Upside-downism: important ingredients for personal fulfilment and a deeper happiness:

- having a strong underlying sense of meaning and purpose in our lives
- security and affirmation in core relationships
- the knowledge that our lives are of benefit to other people.

The professor proceeds to amplify the final point, gesturing to the appropriate place on the screen:

Professor   …and of course we are of benefit to other people in all sorts of different ways…whether face to face…or through what we create, or help to make…or through a service we help to provide
…and whether paid or unpaid.

Reporter (gesturing to the screen)   And what do you think of these *ingredients*, Professor?

Professor   I find them very interesting…
And, you know, this understanding (*gesturing to the screen*) of the sort of things that lead to a deeper happiness and fulfilment ties in very much with some of the findings of contemporary psychology.

Reporter   Well, let me put one final question to you, Professor, if I may.
If there's truth in all of that (*pointing to screen again*), why is it that people's desire to live a materialistic lifestyle remains so very strong?

Professor   That's a fascinating question.
Perhaps part of the reason is that so many people now feel that they have to spend significant sums of money – sometimes extravagant sums of money – in order to advance other parts of their lives
…their need for peer acceptance…esteem…status
…their sexuality
…their desire to live the family dream…
and so on.

Reporter   So, it's not just about spending money and having 'things'
…it's that the need to spend money has penetrated so deeply into other parts of life.

Professor   Precisely…and that's something that Upside-downers have grave misgivings about.

Reporter   We are virtually out of time now.
Thank you so much for talking about Upside-downism to us this evening…although I realize that we've only just scraped the surface.

Image 9

Professor   Yes, don't forget Upside-downism is also about many other issues – including forgiveness… reconciliation…the exercise of power…the service of others.

Reporter   Well, perhaps we'll be able to visit you again some day.
Thank you so much, Professor.
And to everybody who has joined us this evening: thank you for watching, because that's all from
…*The Way We Are Tonight.*

Image 10

The theme tune is played as the professor and the reporter depart.

UPSIDE-DOWN PEOPLE, DRAMA 2: RECONCILIATION AND PEACE

For practicalities, see the introductory section at the start of 'Upside-down people, Drama 1'.

SETTING THE SCENE

In a moment, we are going to watch a short play together. Before the play starts, listen to these sayings of Jesus. They are examples of what is sometimes called his Upside-down teaching.

Image 11

The words on the screen are read out.

Love your enemies instead of hating them.
Don't retaliate or try to get even when people maltreat you. Rather, forgive them … and keep forgiving them.
If somebody slaps you on the right cheek, let him slap your left cheek too.

UPSIDE-DOWN PEOPLE, DRAMA 2: RECONCILIATION AND PEACE

Image 12

The programme's theme tune is played as the professor and the reporter take up their positions.

Reporter   Good evening, and welcome to *The Way We Are Tonight*.

If you're a regular viewer of our programme, you might recall that, a little while ago, we visited the University of Comberford in order to talk with one of its professors – Professor John Jones.

Professor Jones told us something about the Upside-down people. These are men and women who seek to live their lives upside down … they're sometimes known as *Homo sapiens upsidedownus* or *Homo sapiens invertus*.

Image 13

Reporter   So, we're here to meet Professor Jones again in order to hear a little more about the Upside-down people.

Professor, thank you for giving us your time this evening.

Professor   Thank you.

Reporter   Professor, could you just start by reminding us who the Upside-down people are?

Professor   You might remember that Upside-downers are a fairly wide-ranging group. A good number of them are Christians who have been deeply influenced by the moral teaching of Jesus of Nazareth. They believe that we, as human beings, need to turn many of our most common assumptions, many of our received wisdoms, upside down (*motions with his arm*) – through 180 degrees, on their heads – if we are to make genuine progress.

I've actually got something to put up on the screen that might be helpful here.

Image 14

Reporter (*pointing to the screen*)   So, these are some of the issues that Upside-down people are particularly interested in. These are the sorts of areas where they believe familiar values and attitudes often need to be turned upside down.

Professor   Yes, that's right.

The professor proceeds to read Image 14:

Professor   Some key issues for Upside-downism
- Material possessions
- What makes people happy and fulfilled?
- The meaning of power
- The service of others
- Different ways of handling friction
- Forgiveness and reconciliation
- War and peace.

Reporter   Let's cut to the chase here, Professor.

Looking at the issues at the bottom of the page there ...

Are Upside-down people pacifists? Do they believe that the use of military force is always wrong?

Professor   No. Some Upside-downers are pacifists but many are not. A great many Upside-down people believe that military intervention is justified in certain circumstances ... because the most extreme forms of aggression and violence cannot be halted in any other way.

Reporter   So the use of military force is sometimes morally justifiable, but only within the strictest of conditions?

Professor   Yes, indeed ...

But that doesn't really get us to the heart of what Upside-downers want to say here.

Reporter   Please ... go on.

Professor   Upside-down people believe that much of the world's unhappiness is caused by downward cycles of retaliation ... tit-for-tat ... resentment ... suspicion –

whether we are talking about stresses in family relationships ...

gossip and bad feeling in the office ...

or friction between ethnic groups ... or between nation states.

And once these cycles of retaliation and resentment get going, they spiral. They gather momentum. This is something we all recognize.

Reporter   Yes, I'm sure it is.

Professor   What Upside-downism contends is that it nearly always requires a first step of moral courage – of non-retaliation, of attempted peacemaking – if these cycles are to be broken. That's the essence of it.

Image 15

Professor (continuing)   ...and that's precisely what turning the other cheek often is (*gesturing to screen*) ... it's that first step of moral courage to break the downward cycle.

Brief pause

Reporter   So ... Upside-downism here is definitely as much about personal relationships as it is about global relationships.

Professor   Absolutely.

Reporter   Can you say a bit more about that, Professor?

Professor   Well, Upside-downers suggest that, in personal life, there can often be no hope of improved relationships ... no hope of reconciliation ... unless somebody is willing to take this first step of moral courage

... even if it might well be rebuffed

... even if it is a step that might have to be taken on more than one occasion.

Reporter   Okay. I'm sure, again, we all recognize the truth in that. But aren't there sometimes circumstances in which, actually, things need to be brought to a head?

Professor   Yes, of course. But non-retaliation isn't the same as pretending that there isn't a problem. Also ... if we think for a moment about the most difficult of circumstances ... it is important to recognize when a relationship has actually become so damaging that the status quo is simply not an option.

Reporter   Indeed.

Professor   But none of this detracts from the reality that in all areas of life – at home, at work, in the street, at school – Upside-down values are often ones that are desperately needed.

Reporter   Professor, once more, I'm afraid, we've run out of time. Thank you so much for being with us. And to everybody who has joined us this evening: thank you for watching, because that's all from
… *The Way We Are Tonight.*

Image 16

The theme tune is played as the professor and the reporter depart.

YOUR KINGDOM COME

INTRODUCTION

'Your kingdom come' is a short visual reflection exploring the meaning of the kingdom of God in today's world.

PREPARATION

Suggested introductory Bible reading: Matthew 13.31–33.

This item includes a PowerPoint presentation containing photographic images to complement and interpret the text. To download the fully prepared presentation, please go to <www.advent2harvest.co.uk> (see page 1 above). The contents are set out below.

Image 1:   the title ('Your kingdom come')

Image 2:   highlighted biblical text – Matthew 6.10

Image 3:   collage of works of art – the stable, the crucifixion, the empty tomb

Image 4:   the central portion of the Window of the Holy Spirit, St Peter's Basilica, Rome

Image 5:   image of hands (parent and child)

Image 6:   collage – a friendship group; a family group; an isolated child in a school playground; colleagues seated round a table

Images 7 and 8:   collages – a calendar hanging on a wall; a bank statement; a carers and toddlers group; somebody visiting a patient in hospital; emergency food supplies arriving in a drought area

Images 9 and 10:   collages – a factory employee at work on an assembly line; an artist at work; a carer; a farm worker; the door to a headteacher's office or accountant's office; the front cover of the score for one of Bach's Brandenburg Concertos

Images 11 and 12:   collages – William Wilberforce; the Traidcraft logo; a newspaper headline ('Local business woman's ethical stance'); Elizabeth Fry; Martin Luther King; a credit union logo

Image 13:   as Image 1.

YOUR KINGDOM COME

Image 1

The kingdom of God was the central theme of Jesus' teaching.
Over and over again, this was the theme he returned to.
But the kingdom was not just the central theme of Jesus' teaching …
it was the central theme of his life.
He was God's anointed, God's chosen one
… God's king.
His reason for being among us,
his essential purpose,
was to usher in God's kingdom.

Brief pause

Establishing God's kingdom
was not, of course, a matter of securing sovereignty over a particular country or territory.
It was not that sort of a kingdom.

Image 2

The meaning of the kingdom of God is summarized for us in the words of the Lord's
Prayer.
Your kingdom come,
your will be done,
on earth as in heaven.[1]

The kingdom is precisely this:
It is God's will being done on the earth
… as it is in heaven.

The kingdom is God's desire …
God's desire for
love and wholeness,
justice and reconciliation,
becoming a reality.

Pause for reflection

So, Jesus' mission was to usher in God's kingdom … God's reign.

When the pioneering phase of this work was complete …

Image 3

When the foundations had been laid,
Jesus sent his Spirit to us –
to help us to live the life of the kingdom
… and carry on the work of the kingdom.

Image 4

Brief pause

> God's kingdom is yet to be fulfilled.
> It is not yet complete.
>
> But how is the kingdom present in the world now ... today?
>
> The kingdom is present
> when we recognize, and receive, God's affection for us ...

Image 5

> when we know that we are known
> ... known and loved.

Image 6

> The kingdom is among us
> when God's way of love is given expression
> in our relationships with each other ...
>
> ... in the ways in which we treat
> the members of our families, friends and colleagues ... and the friendless.
>
> The kingdom can be a reality
> through the ways in which we handle friction
> ... and seek to foster understanding and togetherness.

Brief pause

> How is God's kingdom present in the world now ... today?

Image 7

> The kingdom can be present in the ways in which we
> use time ...
> spend money ...
> respond to need. *Image 8*

Image 9

> God's kingdom can be a reality through the ways in which we
>
> work ...
> create ...
> imagine. *Image 10*

Image 11

> God's reign can be embraced in the ways in which we participate in public and economic
> life ... and strive for justice and peace. *Image 12*

Pause for reflection

Image 13

> So, Jesus' mission was nothing less than to bring God's reign into the world ...
> into every part of life ...
> into real life.
>
> God's kingdom grows as people respond.
>
> How big is your vision?
> How big is your vision of Jesus and his mission?
> How big is your vision of the work of the Holy Spirit in the world?
> How big is your vision of what it is that Christ calls you to be and to do?

Brief pause

A CLOSING PRAYER

> Lord, we ask you to establish your reign in our hearts and minds.
> Lord, we ask you to empower us by your Spirit to be servants of your kingdom
>   in this complex world.
> Lord, we ask you to equip your Church
> to make known your kingdom ... to bear witness to all that you are doing, and
>   all that you want to do, in your creation.
> Lord, we ask you to fill us with hope for that day when your kingdom will be
>   complete.
> Amen.

Conclusion: the Lord's Prayer

THE PROBLEM OF SUFFERING

INTRODUCTION

'The problem of suffering' combines reflective readings and photographic images to explore this most difficult and heartfelt of issues. It could be used in place of a sermon in various forms of service. The language is never technical but this item will appeal to those who like to reflect a little more deeply about the nature of their faith.

PREPARATION

Bible reading

Within Western thought, the problem of suffering is typically understood as the need to reconcile the existence of a loving and all-powerful God with the reality of the world's pain. If God is all-loving, he must wish to eradicate suffering. If God is omnipotent, he must be able to do so. So why is there so much suffering in the world?

This is the essential logic behind many anguished cries:

How could God allow this to happen?

How can there be a loving God when such terrible things as this occur?

We do not actually find the problem of suffering addressed in quite these philosophical terms in either the Old or New Testaments. Given this, one suggestion for a Bible reading is Philippians 2.5–8. The passage reminds us of the wider theological context within which we discuss the problem of pain. God is not aloof, unfeeling, immune. God suffers too, and, in Christ, has entered into the heart of the human condition.

Photographic images

This item includes a PowerPoint presentation. To download the fully prepared presentation, please go to <www.advent2harvest.co.uk> (see page 1 above). The contents are set out below.

Image 1:   title page ('The problem of suffering')

Image 2:   Van Gogh's despairing man (*On the Threshold of Eternity*)

Image 3:   'Approach One'

Image 4:   A robot

Image 5:   Verbal abuse and humiliation

Image 6:   Physical violence

Image 7:   A 'sweat shop'

Image 8:   Juxtaposition of two pictures – one of a ripened cereal crop, the other depicting starvation

Image 9:   War scene

Image 10: A death camp

Image 11: 'Pause for thought …'

Image 12: 'Approach Two'

Image 13: Picture of John Keats

Image 14: Collage – Malala Yousafzai; an emergency rescue

Image 15: Collage – a kidney donor department; parent and child; Mother Teresa; a child sharing an ice-cream with a friend

Image 16: A 'lived-in' face

Image 17: A photograph of biblical text (Genesis 1.31) with 'it was very good' highlighted

Image 18: Image 11 repeated

Image 19: 'Approach Three'

Image 20: A grandfather clock

Image 21: A model railway

Image 22: Massed vegetation within an equatorial jungle

Image 23: Cells under a microscope

Image 24: A world globe with superimposed symbolism

Image 25: Image 11 repeated

Image 26: Image 1 repeated

Image 27: Salvador Dali, *Christ of St John of the Cross*.

BACKGROUND THEOLOGICAL NOTES

Three distinctive approaches to the problem of suffering are presented here. Each approach is, for obvious reasons, outlined only with the very broadest of brush strokes.

In the notes, I have indicated some relevant background texts.[1]

Given the scale of the world's pain, it might be tempting to resort to the belief that suffering is simply part of the mystery of God and of life: it is not something that we can ever understand, and we need not try.

It is certainly the case that the Church has not provided the sort of comprehensive answer to the problem of suffering that satisfies everybody. However, its theologians have provided us with a range of important and helpful insights and these should not be undervalued. Indeed, there is a grave price to be paid for declaring that the love of God is ultimately mysterious in nature. How, the sceptical linguistic philosophers of the 1950s and 1960s asked, is a love that is *ultimately mysterious* different from no love at all? And, of course, the central tenet of Christian faith is not that God's love for us is fundamentally mysterious – although it may contain elements of mystery – but that it is actually analogous to the love that devoted parents have for their children. The Church needs to continue to present theological understandings that uphold the basic credibility of this analogy through showing that there are circumstances in which omnipotent love and suffering can co-exist.

THE PROBLEM OF SUFFERING

Image 1

How could God allow this to happen?
How can there be a loving God when such terrible things as this can occur?

Image 2

There can't be many of us who haven't at some time felt the full emotional force of these questions – whether in response to a personal tragedy in our own lives or when we have been confronted by horrific headlines in the news.

Christian theologians sometimes refer to this as 'the problem of suffering'.

If God is both all-loving and all-powerful, why is there so much suffering in the world?

The problem of suffering is perhaps the greatest single intellectual obstacle to Christian faith.

During the next few moments, we are going to look briefly at three different approaches to the problem of suffering.

Image 3

For some people, the key to understanding the problem of suffering is human freedom.

Image 4

They argue that God didn't make human beings like robots. He made us with free will so that we could make our own choices. This freedom is an essential dimension of our humanity – an essential part of what it is that makes us human.

But sometimes, we abuse our freedom . . . and this often results in pain. Examples of this are many and varied.

Individuals hurting each other

Image 5

. . . whether emotionally

Image 6

. . . or physically.

Image 7

Economic exploitation . . .

Image 8

Starvation and malnutrition . . . even though we are capable of growing enough food to feed everybody on the planet . . .

Image 9

The aggression that leads to war . . .

Image 10

Clearly, a great deal of the world's pain stems from human wrongdoing. It is a consequence of human beings abusing their freedom.

However, this approach has its limitations. For there are obviously many instances of suffering in the world that don't seem to be caused by human beings in any way at all ... including many forms of disease and physical disaster.[2]

Image 11

Image 12

Image 13

The poet John Keats described the world as a vale of soul-making.[3]
What Keats is saying is that only a world containing some suffering and hardship would allow us the opportunity to truly grow and develop as people.
Consider this for a moment.

Image 14

If there was no danger in the world, then there would be no such thing as courage.

Image 15

And if the world contained an absolute abundance of everything, then there would be no generosity or selflessness.

Image 16

And if there were no challenges or setbacks in life, then there would be no opportunities for the development of perseverance and character.
    courage ...
    selflessness ...
    generosity ...
    moral character ...
    They just wouldn't exist.
    Human existence would be unrecognizable. We would have lost whole layers of depth and meaning from our lives.
    If there were no hardships and challenges – or if God always intervened to sweep our difficulties aside – then human life would be of a totally different order.

Image 17

This has even led some Christian writers to suggest that God's world is *good* in a highly specific sense. The world is good in the sense that it is fit for a very important purpose. It is the right sort of environment for *soul-making* – for giving people the opportunity to grow and develop as people.

There are undoubtedly some important insights within this second approach. But some suffering is so awful ... so crushing ... that it is very hard to see it as all part of God's master plan.[4]

Image 18

Image 19

The first approach focused on the suffering that is caused through human wrongdoing.

The second approach focused on the character of suffering – and on the complex and profound part it plays in human life.

The third approach focuses on the way in which God creates.

Image 20

Think about a grandfather clock.

It is a wonderful piece of craftsmanship. It runs beautifully. But it has been made to run in just one pre-set way. The way it operates is wholly pre-determined.

Image 21

Or, similarly, think about a magnificent model railway.

Again, it runs beautifully. But it too can only run in certain pre-programmed ways.

Image 22

But perhaps the creation isn't like a grandfather clock or a model railway. Perhaps God created the material world in such a manner that it had some capacity to develop in its own way ... so that it wouldn't just be a rigid extension of himself.

If this sort of understanding is correct then we do not live in a world where every aspect of existence – where every change and development in the natural order – has been wholly pre-determined from the very outset.

Image 23

But if the material world genuinely possesses some degree of potential – some capacity – to develop in its own way

...then it must also possess some potential to develop elements of disorder

...and this might explain, for example, the emergence of disease and other dysfunctions.

Indeed, perhaps any form of creation – that isn't just a simple rigid extension of its creator – must have within it some potential to *fall away*.

Brief pause

Image 24

But God is not passive in the face of the world's sufferings.

Image 25

Image 26

There is a limit to what human beings can understand. Indeed, all great systems of knowledge and belief have their gaps and apparent contradictions ... the things that they can't explain.

As Christians, we probably do not possess the sort of comprehensive answer to the problem of suffering that will satisfy everybody. Each of these three approaches offers us important insights but also leaves us with questions. Perhaps each of them is a part of the answer.

Brief pause

Image 27

CLOSING PRAYER

And when human hearts are breaking
under sorrow's iron rod,
then they find that self-same aching
deep within the heart of God.[5]

Lord, there is so much that we don't understand.
But you are not distant or unfeeling.
You share in the world's pain.
You have borne our frailties and our flaws on the cross;
and when we suffer, you suffer too.

Strengthen our faith.
And help us to work with you
…to be instruments of your compassion,
and channels of your healing,
in this world of beauty and brokenness.
Amen.

GAZUMPED!

A drama in celebration of the Fairtrade movement

INTRODUCTION

'Gazumped!' uses humour to develop its theme.

While this item can obviously be used at any time of the year, do note that Fairtrade Fortnight usually takes place in February.

PREPARATION

The sketch has a very simple format. The context is a TV game show.

Participants

- Two or three readers for the introductory and concluding sections
- The game show host
- Two contestants
- The stage assistant (and backstage voice)
- An organist or keyboard player.

If you are unable to provide live music, it will not be difficult to utilize pre-recorded music and improvise sound effects.

Only a few simple props are required.

It might be an idea for the host to carry an iPad for prompts.

ORGANIZATIONS

There are a number of important organizations working in this area. Two of them are:

- Fairtrade Foundation: <www.fairtrade.org.uk>
- Traidcraft: <www.traidcraft.co.uk>

These organizations produce a range of publicity materials providing statistical information, answers to frequently asked questions, stories, activities . . .

GAZUMPED!

INTRODUCTION

Reader 1   The Bible tells us that God cares deeply about how we treat one another.

Reader 2   He cares about the ways in which we treat our families, friends, neighbours, work colleagues . . . and the strangers we meet.

Reader 3   And God is also concerned about how we treat those people whose lives we touch through our economic activities.

    The Old Testament prophets cried out against the economic injustices that they saw in their communities. And Jesus said that when we reach out to the poor and the disadvantaged, we are also reaching out to him.[1]

Reader 1   There is a saying in the Old Testament book of Proverbs: 'Accuracy of scales and balances is the LORD's concern; all the weights in the bag are God's business.'[2]

Reader 2   Or, as another version of the Bible puts it: 'The LORD wants every sale to be fair.'[3]

Reader 3   The saying has implications for our various economic roles – including our role as consumers. When we purchase goods or services, it matters to God that those who have been involved in providing for us in this way have been fairly rewarded.

Reader 1   Yet many millions of people in the world today are condemned to poverty because a fair price is not being paid for the goods they make or the food that they grow. However hard they work, they are always up against it because such low prices are paid for their product in local or world markets. This form of economic injustice is a major cause of global poverty – but it is there in the history of many of the items that appear on the shelves in our shops.

Reader 2   This is why the Fairtrade movement is so important. When we buy Fairtrade goods, we know that those who produced them have been fairly treated – both financially and in terms of their working conditions.

Reader 3   We are now going to watch a short play.

THE DRAMA

A voice 'backstage'   Ladies and gentleman, please welcome with a round of applause your host
for this evening … Joe Just.

The host enters to music played by the organist.

Host   Thank you, thank you, and welcome to TV's most dramatic quiz show … *Gazumped!*
The show where knowing the answers is not enough to take home the big prize.

The music continues for a few seconds while the host does a little jig.

Host   Without any further ado, let's give a big hand to today's two contestants … Rosie and
Michael.

The contestants enter to music.

Host   So, Rosie, are you looking forward to playing *Gazumped!* this evening?
Rosie   Yes. I'm a bit nervous but basically, yes … yes, I'm very excited.
Host   Excellent, excellent. And who is in the audience with you, Rosie?
Rosie   My fiancé, Dave. We're saving up to buy a house.
Host   You're saving up to buy a house! So tonight's quiz could be very helpful. Let's hope
it is.
And Michael, welcome to you too.
Michael   Thank you, Joe.
Host   Well, Michael, have you been working hard on tonight's topic which, as you know, is
'Shopping Around the World'?
Michael   Yes, I have. I've been working quite hard really.
Host   Excellent, excellent.
And who is in the audience supporting you?
Michael   My wife, Jackie and our eldest child, Ben.
Host   Good, good.
Ladies and gentlemen, there are two sounds that you need to listen out for during
the show.

The organist plays a few 'celebratory' notes.

Host   When we hear that music, we know that one of our contestants has hit the jackpot.

The organist plays notes indicative of bad news.

Host   Now let's hope, we don't hear that sound this evening. Because that sound means
that one of our contestants has been gazumped. And we don't want that, do we?
Rosie, you have the first question. So let's see how much the first question could
be worth to you.

The stage assistant enters holding up a large card showing '£15,000'.

Host   That's good, Rosie. That's very good.
Here's the question … for £15,000.
It has been estimated that the people of the United Kingdom drink over
150 million cups of tea each day. But in which century was tea first introduced
in this country?

At these points in the quiz, the host and contestant ad lib a little: the host repeating the question, the contestant ruminating out loud about possible answers, etc. Or the contestant might just take time to think. However, it is also important to keep the quiz moving along.

Rosie   I'm going to say … the seventeenth century.

Host   A round of applause, please. The seventeenth century is the correct answer.
               Excellent, excellent!
               So, Michael, here's your question. Let's see if we can get you off to a good start too.

The assistant brings in a card showing '£4,000'.

Host   That's not bad. It could get you off to a nice solid start.
               This is your question … for £4,000.
               It's a chocolate-tasting question.
               We're going to put a blindfold on you, Michael. We're then going to hand you a plate with a piece of chocolate on it. You need to tell me whether the chocolate is
               1 Cadbury's
               2 Galaxy, or
               3 Green and Black's.

The assistant puts a blindfold on Michael. He eats the chocolate and pauses for a moment.

Michael   I do like chocolate. I think that's Green and Black's.

Host   Well done! Well done, indeed! That's the correct answer.

Host encourages applause. The blindfold is taken off.

Host   What a wonderful start! Two correct answers.
               Back to you, Rosie.

The assistant enters holding up a card showing '£50,000'. The organist plays the jackpot music.

Host   Oh! Wonderful, wonderful! Rosie, you have the jackpot card. You now have the chance to win a further £50,000.
               I want you to just take a little time … one or two deep breaths.
               Okay … here's your question … for the jackpot.
               It's one of our favourite 'What am I?' questions …
               I am *gossypium*. *(Host spells.)*
               I am one of the biggest *non-food* crops on the planet.
               In many countries in the world, growers *or manufacturers*, and their workers, depend on me for their livelihood.
               I am not a tree.
               What am I?

Ad lib

Rosie   I'm pretty sure, Joe, that the answer is cotton.

Host   Yes! That is the correct answer.

The organist plays the jackpot music. The host encourages applause.

Host   Rosie, you now have a grand total of £65.000. Excellent, excellent.
               Michael, let's see if we can move things along for you. How much is your next question going to be worth?

The organist plays the notes indicating a gazump.

Host   Oh, no! No ... no ... no!! I'm afraid you've been gazumped.

The assistant brings on a large envelope, opens it and passes the contents to the host. He reads for a moment.

Host   This is a little bit tricky, Michael. If you choose to take this on, you will need to try to answer your question before you know how much it is worth. Okay?
    Now, I can tell you, it could be worth £10,000 or ... it could be worth £2,000 or ... it could be worth minus – that's minus – £6,000.
    All right?
    But you have a choice. You can just pass on this round and accept a nil return.
However, if you go ahead, you could end up, as it were, selling at a loss.
    It is entirely your choice, Michael. What do you want to do?

Michael (after a little hesitation) I'll take it on, Joe.

Host   Brave man, brave man. A round of applause, ladies and gentlemen.
Here's your question. It's another 'What am I?' ...
I am one of the biggest *food crops* in the world.
I share my name with a secretary of state in the administration of President George W. Bush.
What am I?

Ad lib

Michael   My answer is rice.

Host   A round of applause. 'Rice' is correct.
So, now let's see how much you've won.

The assistant brings on a card showing '–£6,000' (minus £6,000).

Host   Oh, that's rotten. That's not good at all. But there is still time, Michael ... still time.
Now, let's just take a minute to look at our running totals.
Rosie, you have a very nice £65,000.
But Michael, you owe *us* £2,000. But, as I say, there's still time.
Let's go back to you, Rosie, for your next question.
But let me ask you first, are you enjoying the game this evening?

Rosie   Yes, I am enjoying it, but ... well, it does seem, you know, a bit unfair.

Host (putting a hand on her arm)   Don't worry about that, you just need to focus on your own game.
Let's have your final question.

A card is shown for '£5,000'.

Host   Another solid card.
So, your final question.
Coffee is big business. It is served in many ways. But if you'd ordered a mocha ... a mocha ... what would you be drinking?

Brief ad lib

Rosie   Espresso coffee, chocolate and hot milk.

Host   That's correct, Rosie.

Applause

Host	And that gives you a total prize of £70,000.
	Excellent, excellent. That is really terrific.
	Now Michael, let's see if we can turn things around for you. Here's your final card.

A card is shown for '£8,000'.

Host	Michael, this could get you back in the black.
	Here's the question.
	I am one of the most popular fruits in the world.
	I am grown in huge quantities in the tropics.
	I gave my name to a pop band who were big in the 1980s.
	What am I?

Ad lib

Michael	I think the answer is bananas. That's my answer.
Host	That's correct …

The organist plays the notes indicating a gazump.

Host	No! No, no, no!! … not again!

The assistant brings an envelope to the host and opens it. The host reads the contents.

Host	Michael, I can tell you that this is not too bad. You're not going to lose any more money. But you do have to answer another question to actually get your hands on the £8,000 which you have just won. You've got to answer one more question. Okay? *(Michael nods.)*
	My beautiful wife and I have just splashed out on a boat for our holidays in the Greek islands. Splashed out … new boat … no pun intended!!
	So here's the question:

Pause

Host *(with just the slightest touch of edge in his voice)*	How much did we pay for the boat?
Michael *(looking disorientated)*	I don't know. I just haven't a clue.
Host	How much did we pay for the boat. I need an answer.
Michael	I'll just have to take a wild guess. I don't know … I'll say … £500,000.
Host	Oh, Michael, I am sorry – that's a long way short.
	Ladies and gentlemen, what a shame!
	And I'm afraid that brings us to the end of the show. Please give a big round of applause to our two terrific contestants.

Music plays. Host and contestants exit.

CONCLUSION

Reader 1   The play is, perhaps, a rather unlikely and extreme parable. But for very many people in the world today, real life is rather like being Michael in *Gazumped!* However hard they work, however well they work, they are always up against it because a fair price is not being paid for the food they grow or the goods they produce. So they and their families are trapped in poverty.

Reader 2   This is why buying Fairtrade goods can help to make a real difference to people's lives.

Reader 3   Many millions of people are economically dependent on the production of rice, tea, coffee, chocolate, bananas, cotton … We can now buy all of these products – and many more – through Fairtrade arrangements.

Reader 1   Of course, the economics of trade are immensely complicated. There has to be an authentic demand for what is grown or made. And it is sometimes not easy to say what, exactly, a just price is. But powerful buyers can drive prices down to levels that are a long way from being fair and that are highly damaging to producers and their workers.

　　The lesson of history is that conventional forms of trade have always tended to discriminate against the poorest and the weakest.[4]

Reader 2   But what God requires is justice. All the weights in the bag are God's business.

A SERVICE FOR THE LOCAL COMMUNITY

INTRODUCTION

This is a short, accessible service for members of the wider community.

Alongside easy-to-sing hymns, the service incorporates:

1 a visual act of thanksgiving for those who serve *us* within the community

2 a short visual reading on the nature of human togetherness

3 prayers

4 other musical items.

PREPARATION

Invitations

Invitations could be sent to shops and businesses, charities, local clubs and organizations, other churches and faith communities, local councillors and officials, representatives of schools, colleges, youth organizations, etc. Important decisions need to be taken in this respect. How formal should the invitations be? Should they include an RSVP?

Act of Thanksgiving

The text for the Act of Thanksgiving (see script) depicts the many and varied ways in which we serve each other within the local community. The visual accompaniment to this text can be provided in a number of ways:

- The text for the Act of Thanksgiving is read. After each paragraph (that is, after each form of service has been introduced), a small group of people – representing this particular way of serving the community – process through the congregation to the front of the church. As they come forward, they carry the tools of their trade or other pointers to the service they provide, or they could be wearing uniform or other indicative clothing. For example:

  - a district nurse, scout leader, police officer, railway worker . . . in uniform

  - a builder, mechanic, window cleaner, member of the highways maintenance team or park grounds staff . . . carrying tools

  - a local councillor wearing the chain of office, the owner of a local business bearing the company's product

- a waiter or waitress carrying a tray with food or drink

- a librarian with a pile of books

- a hairdresser with scissors, mirror and spray

- a representative from the Citizens Advice Bureau carrying a placard with CAB on it

- a member of a shop's staff with a basket containing merchandise.

My advice would be that you should only take up this option if you have the time and resources available to handle the organization involved – the procession could easily include upwards of 20 people – and the personal sensitivities that can arise.

• The text for the Act of Thanksgiving is read. After each form of service has been introduced, a selection of objects is brought forward to the front of the church. The objects portray or symbolize this particular way of serving the community; the previous paragraph offers some ideas. The various objects are arranged to create a montage of community service. This is much simpler to organize than the previous option. One small group of people, possibly a group of youngsters, could be asked to undertake the task of presenting and arranging all the constituent items of the montage. This approach also has the advantage of creating a visual effect that lasts throughout the service. However, it can still be tricky ensuring that no groups of people or organizations feel excluded.

• The third format is probably the simplest in terms of preparation and organization. A particular reason for its adoption here is that it synchronizes so well with the rest of the service. The text for the Act of Thanksgiving is read as in the other options. After each form of service has been introduced, a block (wrapped cardboard box), bearing a large capital letter, is brought to the front of the church and placed in position. The letters eventually form the word TOGETHER (see below).

Music

I have suggested three contemporary hymns which, in my experience, have always worked well in these sorts of contexts. However, local knowledge is always important in relation to these choices.

You might like to consider incorporating some form of live music for the congregation to listen to during the service. This could be provided by a school choir, a church choir or, perhaps, by a local folk group or singing group. The choice obviously needs to be made with care. My personal feeling is that it is not necessary for the choir or group to be restricted to songs that have their specific origins within the Christian community provided that what is sung expresses something of the spirit of Christian values and community life. The choices that are agreed will, of course, reflect the choir or group's repertoire. However, I have suggested that the song 'He ain't heavy, he's my brother' (B. Scott and B. Russell) would be particularly appropriate after the Bible reading.

A SERVICE FOR THE LOCAL COMMUNITY

INTRODUCTION AND WELCOME

Hymn: 'Colours of day'

THE ACT OF THANKSGIVING

We now come to our Act of Thanksgiving. We are going to give thanks for all those people who work hard for us and seek to do their best to serve us within our community. We serve each other in many different ways. Some of them are paid, some of them are unpaid. Some of the ways in which we serve each other are highly visible, others are hardly visible at all. But they are all important.

We start by thanking God for those within the community who are especially important to us – the members of our families ... our friends ... good neighbours ...

The first E in TOGETHER is brought to the front of the church and placed in position – see introduction.

We thank God for others who care for us when we are vulnerable: for those
... who work in the medical professions
... or in the emergency services
... or who make time for us ... to listen to us ... to guide us.
We thank God for those who raise funds to support those in need, in the community and elsewhere.

The second E is brought to the front of the church and placed in position.

And we give thanks for those who teach and nurture
... who bring inspiration into our lives
... who help to create special places of belonging
through clubs and societies,
through art, drama, sport, music,
through our schools and colleges, the library and museum,
through places where we can just sit and chat, and have something to eat or drink.

The second T is brought forward and placed in position.

We thank God for those who provide colour for us through their gardens;
and for those who look after the open spaces where we can walk ... run ... play.

The O

We give thanks for those who generate economic activity within our community
... who help to create jobs
... who provide us with our homes, and help us to maintain them
... who provide us with the goods that we need,
and with the many services that we require.

The H and the R

> And we thank God for those who work hard to offer leadership,
> and for those who create and maintain
> essential forms of social organization
> … our legal system
> … our economic infrastructure: transport, roads, water, drains, refuse disposal,
> communications and utilities.

The final letters: the first T and the G

Service sheet/screen

> Lord, we thank you for our community of …
> We thank you for each and every person who serves us here.

All: **We could not do without them.**

Choir/singing group: item 1

Bible reading: 1 Corinthians 13.1–8a, 13

Choir/singing group: item 2, 'He ain't heavy, he's my brother'

Reader(s)   We are going to have a short reading now about the importance of togetherness
in human life – whether we are thinking about families, friendship groups, the places
where we work alongside others, local and national communities or, ultimately, the
whole human family.

Pause

> No person is an island.
> We are as dependent on each other as we are on the air that we breathe.
> God made us to be social creatures.
> He wanted us to know the joy of belonging.
> He wanted us to know the security of belonging.
> He wanted us to know the deep sense of fulfilment that comes through serving
> others.
> He wanted us to be able to harness the creative energy and the mutual support that
> come from doing things together.

Pause

> We are better together;
> because in true togetherness the whole is always greater than the sum of the parts.
>
> But togetherness has many enemies:
> snobbery … envy … arrogance … gossip …

Two of the letters in TOGETHER are removed.

> a lack of awareness of the needs and feelings of others

Two further letters are removed.

> … prejudice … crime

Two further letters are removed.

> ... economic injustice ... unfairness in politics.

The two final letters are removed.

Pause

> On the other hand, togetherness is strengthened
> by honesty and integrity ... they are building blocks of trust

Two of the letters are restored.

> ... by the strong empowering the vulnerable

Two further letters are restored.

> ... by people who are willing to go the extra mile ... and people who are peacemakers

Two further letters are restored.

> ... by forgiveness ... kindness ... respect
> ... commitment in relationships.

The two final letters are restored.

> Community is not only a precious gift,
> it is an awesome responsibility.
> Relationships can never be taken for granted,
> they need to be constantly nurtured.

Pause

> Loving God, forgiving God,
> help us, whenever we can,
> to be builders of community
> and creators of togetherness.
> Amen.

Hymn: 'Brother, sister, let me serve you'

PRAYERS

As we pray, it is important to remember that God is not aloof or unfeeling. In Jesus, God lived among us, as one of us. He became part of a human community. As a man, he experienced all the ups and downs of human life. So, knowing God's love for us – and his interest in us – we can pray to him now.

We start by praying for those who are close to us.

Perhaps there are people known to us who are in particular need of our prayers at this time – perhaps because of illness, or bereavement, or worries about family or money or work . . . whatever it is.

In the quietness, we focus our thoughts on them . . . *(pause)*

Lord God, we commit to you each person we have thought about . . . *(pause)*

Hold them in your care.

Encircle them with your love,

now and for ever.

Amen.

And we pray for ourselves.

Perhaps we are facing particular difficulties or anxieties at the present time.

In the quietness, we focus, for a moment, on our own lives . . . *(pause)*

Lord God, hold us in your care . . . *(pause)*

Show us the right path ahead.

Encircle us with your love,

now and for ever.

Amen.

At this point there is an opportunity for prayer in relation to any particular needs within the community or further afield.

Service sheet/screen

Jesus taught that God's love for us is like the love that devoted parents have for their children. So we pray:

The Lord's Prayer

Choir/singing group: item 3

Notices, expressions of gratitude

Hymn: 'One more step along the world I go'

Blessing

COMPLEX LIVES

A meditation

'Complex lives' is a resource for a short period of quiet reflection. It is suitable for those contexts that require a meditative form of input. The material could be used at any time of the year but it is perhaps particularly appropriate for times of self-examination, including Lent and Advent.

Suggested Bible reading: Psalm 139.1–16.

HANDOUTS

You might like to consider supporting the *spoken word* by producing a handout containing the text of the meditation. If so, please see the introductory section ('Handouts') on page 2.

COMPLEX LIVES

God wanted a world where there could be
a depth of emotional life ...
where there could be
the deep bonds of friendship ...
the appreciation and development of community ...
the experience of love ...
the growth of personality and character.
But these precious realities can only be brought about by and through freedom.
Without freedom they cannot exist.

God wanted a world where there could be joy ...
happiness with substance to it.
God wanted a world where there could be
the journey of faith ...
the accumulation of knowledge and ingenuity ...
the appreciation of beauty ...
the creation of beauty.
But these precious realities can only be brought about by and through freedom.
Without freedom they cannot exist.

Pause for reflection

But human life,
life with freedom,
is a complex experience.

Human life,
life with freedom,
life with questions about identity and goals,
life with issues of self-worth, right and wrong ... and mortality,
is full of complexities.

For most of us, our complexities are many and varied and deep.
For most of us, there are mixed motives in much of what we do;
and our lives often seem to hover back and forth between
confidence and insecurity,
meaning and melancholy
... nobility and shame.[1]

But God knows us.
He knows us better than we know ourselves.
He knows our complexities
... and his love reaches through them.

Pause for reflection

> God knows us.
> He knows us better than we know ourselves.
> As the psalmist put it:
> God knew us before we were
> …he understands all our thoughts
> …and he knows our words before we speak them.[2]

> The thought of God's deep knowledge of the working of our minds,
> and the churning of our hearts,
> might be disturbing
> …but it can also be profoundly reassuring.
> For God knows not only what we are
> but why we are what we are.

> He knows the story of each one of us … the full story.
> He knows the forces,
> from without and within,
> that make us churn.
> He knows the forces,
> from without and within,
> that together forge those 'particular temptations'
> …the ones that assault us with the greatest ferocity,
> or creep up on us most insidiously.

Pause for reflection

> Perfect love drives out all fear.[3]

> The opposite of love can be many things:
> apathy, self-absorption, hatred …
> But so often,
> perhaps most often,
> the opposite of love is actually fear.
> So often, it is our personal insecurities
> …our nagging demons
> that make it hard for us to love.
> And so we are tempted
> to build up layers of self-protectiveness and defensiveness …
> to be prickly and panicky …
> to overreact …
> or even to get our own retaliation in first!

Pause for reflection

CLOSING PRAYER

Lord,
amid the complexities of life,
help us to be grounded in your unconditional love for us ...
and in your perfect knowledge of us.
Save us from complacency or defeatism.
May we never accept that within us which is not of love.
Rather, may we always be open to the Spirit of Love
who casts out fear
and helps us to overcome our temptations.
This we ask in Jesus' name.
Amen.

A short period for silent prayer

REFERENCES

Advent revisited

1 Psalm 8.5 (Revised English Bible).

2 These issues are also explored in 'Harvest: A twenty-first-century celebration of the Creator, creation and creativity'.

3 From *Common Worship: Services and Prayers for the Church of England* (Eucharistic Prayer G). The extract from *Common Worship: Services and Prayers* is copyright © The Archbishops' Council, 2000, and is reproduced by permission. All rights reserved. <copyright©churchofengland.org>. The assertion of the distinctiveness of humankind does not contradict the fact that we share much in common with other animals; and it does not diminish our God-given responsibility to respect and care for them.

4 The concepts and images that contribute in some way to the New Testament picture of the *outcome of the human story* are wide-ranging: triumphal return and reign, sharing God's home, resurrection, judgement, etc. A single notion – such as completion – cannot, of course, do full justice to all of these ideas.

5 Jude 24–25 (adapted).

6 From *The Alternative Service Book* (seventeenth Sunday after Trinity). The extract from *The Alternative Service Book 1980* is copyright © The Archbishops' Council, 1980, and is reproduced by permission. All rights reserved. <copyright©churchofengland.org>.

Christmas and Epiphany tableau

1 Francis Dewar develops this theme of personal calling in a very helpful way in *Called or Collared* (London: SPCK, 1991).

Drama for Lent: The Pharisee and the tax collector

1 The wording of the parable has been taken from the Good News Bible. It has been very slightly modified for dramatic purposes.

2 Matthew 6.5.

3 Matthew 7.1–2.

4 Matthew 7.3–5.

5 Rowan Williams, *Faith in the Public Square* (London: Bloomsbury, 2012), pp. 85–6.

6 Luke 10.25–37.

Palm Sunday procession

1 Matthew 21.5 (Revised English Bible).

2 Matthew 12.20 (adapted).

Good Friday meditation: To the foot of the cross

1 See, for example: William Barclay, *Crucified and Crowned* (London: SCM Press, 1961), p. 91ff; The Doctrine Commission of the General Synod of the Church of England, *The Mystery of Salvation*, Contemporary Doctrine Classics (London: Church House Publishing, 2005), p. 344f; Keith Ward, *Christianity: A Short Introduction* (Oxford: Oneworld Publications, 2000), p. 56ff.

2 The phrase, in this context, comes from Bishop Ian Ramsey in *Religious Language* (London: SCM Press, 1957).

3 I am indebted to the authors of *The Mystery of Salvation* for the suggestion of this particular analogy (p. 362) – although there it is used in a slightly different context.

Pentecost: The Spirit of Jesus

1 Romans 5.5 (Good News Bible).

2 Galatians 5.22–23a (Good News Bible).

3 The subject of the work of the Holy Spirit outside the Church is a complex one. See, for example: The Doctrine Commission of the General Synod of the Church of England, *We Believe in the Holy Spirit*, Contemporary Doctrine Classics (London: Church House Publishing, 2005), p. 141.

Harvest: A twenty-first-century celebration of the Creator, creation and creativity

1 The key text is Genesis 1.26–28.

2 See Gerhard von Rad, *Genesis* (Philadelphia: Westminster, 1961).

3 These particular issues are also explored in 'Advent revisited' (p. 5).

Remembrance Sunday: Lord, are you tempted to intervene?

1 This line is adapted from the song 'Let there be peace on earth' (words: Miller and Jackson, 1955).

Upside-down people, Drama 1: Material possessions and happiness

1 The sayings of Jesus have been adapted from the following sources: Mark 8.34–35; Matthew 5.43–44; Matthew 18.21–22; Matthew 5.38–39 (*Good News Bible*); Matthew 6.19–20; Luke 12.32–34; Acts 20.35; Mark 10.42–45.

2 John Stott, *Christian Counter-culture: The message of the Sermon on the Mount* (Leicester: Inter-Varsity Press, 1978). It has been quite common for writers to refer to Christ's kingdom as an *Upside-down kingdom*.

Your kingdom come

3 Matthew 6.10 (Revised English Bible).

The problem of suffering

1 Jeff Astley, *God's World* (London: Darton, Longman and Todd, 2000). John Hick, *Evil and the God of Love* (London: Collins, 1968); this is a major work in terms of mapping the responses which the Church's theologians have made to the problem of suffering and related issues over the centuries. Keith Ward, *Christianity: A Short Introduction* (Oxford: Oneworld Publications, 2000).

2 By way of interpretation of Genesis 3, some writers understand particular aspects of physical suffering as God's punishment for human sinfulness. See John Hick, *Evil and the God of Love*, p. 178ff.

3 See John Hick, *Evil and the God of Love*, p. 295.

4 The point being made in 'Approach Two' is that human growth requires a certain sort of environment. The suggestion is not that all of our individual sufferings come to us at God's specific direction.

5 The hymn is 'God is love: let heaven adore him' by Timothy Rees.

Gazumped!

1 Matthew 25.37f.

2 Proverbs 16.11 (Revised English Bible).

3 Good News Bible.

4 See FAQs on the Fairtrade Foundation website, <www.fairtrade.org.uk>.

Complex lives

1 Within a reflection of this form, there are inevitably some philosophical presuppositions about the nature of human freedom. A theoretical distinction could, perhaps, be made between the complexities that are inherent in freedom itself and those additional complexities that enter our lives when freedom is abused. Similarly, insecurity, melancholy and shame are clearly not realities that all belong to the same moral or psychological order.

2 Psalm 139.1–16.

3 This is a quotation from 1 John 4.18, although there the underlying theme is different from the one developed within the reflection.